# BIBLE PROBLEMS EXPLAINED

# BIBLE PROBLEMS EXPLAINED

*By* JAMES M. GRAY, D.D.
DEAN OF THE MOODY BIBLE INSTITUTE OF CHICAGO

Author of "How to Master the English Bible," "Synthetic Bible Studies," "Primers of the Faith," "The Antidote to Christian Science," "Satan and the Saint," "Great Epochs of Sacred History," "Salvation from Start to Finish," "Progress in the Life to Come," etc.

> "And Philip said, Understandest thou what thou readest? And he said, How can I except some man should guide me?"
> —*Acts 8:30, 31*

WIPF & STOCK · Eugene, Oregon

Wipf and Stock Publishers
199 W 8th Ave, Suite 3
Eugene, OR 97401

Bible Problems Explained
By Gray, James M.
ISBN 13: 978-1-5326-8462-3
Publication date 3/13/2019
Previously published by Fleming H. Revell, Co., 1913

## PUBLISHER'S NOTE

In common with other Christian ministers, the author for years has been in receipt of questions from correspondents bearing on the problems of the Bible and the Christian life. They have been responded to in the columns of periodicals with which he has been connected, and a number are here gathered together for further use. The frequent employment of the personal pronoun is explained by the circumstance that so many of the questions were addressed to him personally, saying, "What do you think?" etc. It did not seem desirable to change the form of the answers for the purpose of this book. There has been added an index of subjects and Bible texts, which the reader will find valuable.

## CONTENTS

| Chapter | | Page |
|---|---|---|
| | Questions on— | |
| I. | The Bible | 9 |
| II. | The Doctrine of God | 23 |
| III. | The Person of Christ | 29 |
| IV. | The Church | 38 |
| V. | The Christian Ministry | 48 |
| VI. | Christian Doctrine and Life | 53 |
| VII. | Applied Christianity | 78 |
| VIII. | The Future Life | 91 |
| IX. | Israel, or the Jews | 104 |
| X. | Second Coming of Christ and the Millennium | 109 |
| XI. | Satan, Angelology and Modern "Isms" | 117 |

[For "Subject Index" and "Index to Bible Texts," see pages 125 to 128.]

# CHAPTER I.

## QUESTIONS ON THE BIBLE.

**Where shall I find the most terse statement respecting the canon of the Old Testament?**

The strongest witness to the canon of the Old Testament is our Lord Jesus Christ. There is no question but that the Old Testament of His day is the Old Testament of the present. To Him that was the sacred Scriptures—no more, no less. A more authoritative critic than He we can not have.

When we go back of Christ we are following tradition merely. This tradition gives Ezra the final word as to the make-up of the Old Testament books. All scholars have been agreed, with practically few exceptions, up to the present, that it is to him, under God, we owe the literary form of these books.

It is impossible to say in detail who all the writers were, with the exception, of course, of Moses, Ezra, David, Solomon, and the prophets whose names are associated with their different books, and who, for the most part, are recorded as their writers. The most terse statement on the subject will probably be discovered in one of the evangelical Bible dictionaries, like that of Smith or Davis. We might suggest also, *The Historic Origin of the Bible*, by Prof. Bissell.

**Is there any positive proof that the Bible is authentic? If so, what is that proof?**

There is very positive proof of this fact, but it is that which is addressed to faith rather than the reason of unregenerate man. It is quite sufficient to satisfy any unprejudiced and spiritually-enlightened mind, but the natural man is neither unprejudiced nor spiritually-enlightened.

We trace the history of the Bible, just as we do that of another book, from century to century to its source. To speak only of the New Testament, our first printed copy of that sacred volume dates from about the fifteenth century of the Christian era. Back of this printed volume we have manuscripts, some of which are in existence today, of a date as early as the fourth century of the Christian era. While beyond this there is the evidence of versions or translations of these manuscripts, carrying us back to within a period of about fifty years of the death of John, the last of the twelve apostles.

If, therefore, the books we now call the New Testament existed collectively as early as this, the inference is clear that they must have existed separately for a long time previously. But fifty years is not a long time, so that we see there can be no doubt that the books were in existence in the apostolic days, and hence, that they are genuine and authentic.

The Old Testament can be traced in precisely the same way, and to a period two hundred or three hundred years before Christ. But it is not necessary to trace the Old Testament further back than Christ, since it was well known that it was in His hands, and used by Him, just as we have it today. An Old Testament that was sufficiently authentic for our Lord ought to be for us.

**Considering that the Bible during the dark ages passed through the hands of the Catholic priesthood, what evidence have we that it is the same today as when it came from the hands of the apostles?**

The dark ages, and with them the Roman Catholic Church, did not come into existence before the sixth century of the Christian era; but the New Testament, to say nothing of the Old, had been in existence five centuries before. It was in manuscript form, and thousands upon thousands of these manuscripts were scattered throughout the private and public libraries of Europe and Asia. It was the presence of the Bible in this form that enabled a constant protest to be

*The Bible*

kept up against the Roman Catholic Church even throughout the dark ages.

Moreover, some of these old manuscripts are still in existence, one in the British Museum, London, another in the University library at Paris, a third in the Royal library at St. Petersburg, a fourth in the Vatican library at Rome. These manuscripts all agree, and demonstrate that the Roman Catholic Church has not changed the text of the sacred Scriptures in any serious way. The Roman Catholic Bible is all right enough. The trouble is with the Roman Catholics themselves, who, like the pharisaic Jews of our Savior's time, make it "of none effect through their traditions."

## Is the theory of the verbal inspiration of the Scriptures tenable in view of certain apparent contradictions?

The verbal inspiration of the sacred Scriptures is not a theory but a fact. More than two thousand times in the Old Testament do the holy writers introduce their messages with the phrase, "Thus saith the Holy Ghost," or its equivalent. Now, to deny that the Holy Ghost speaks at all in the Scriptures is an intelligible proposition, but to admit that He speaks it is necessary to admit that we have His words, for otherwise how should we know what He says? Compare here 2 Samuel 23:2; Jeremiah 1:9; 1 Corinthians 2:13; 2 Timothy 3:16; 2 Peter 1:21.

Of course, when we speak of verbal inspiration we refer to the original autographs of the Scriptures as they came from the sacred writers, and not to any translation of them. It is the province of Biblical criticism by an examination of the various translations, versions and other data to get at the exact text of the original; and so thoroughly and satisfactorily has this been done that a good authority declares that so far as the New Testament is concerned, we have in nine hundred and ninety-nine cases out of every thousand the very words of the original autographs.

Furthermore, when we speak of verbal inspiration we do

not mean that every word in the Bible is God's own word in the sense that He either uttered it, or caused it to be uttered. On the contrary, there are words of Satan there, and words of human enemies of God, and words of some of His people who spake foolishly. What is meant is that the record in every instance is an inspired record. In other words, we know that God spake thus and so in this case, and some other person thus and so in that case, because God declares it to be a fact in the inspired record He has given us thereof.

Now for the "contradictions" of which the correspondent writes. In Peter's "confession," Mark makes him say "the Christ"; Luke, "the Christ of God"; and Matthew, "the Christ, the Son of the living God." This seems an insuperable objection to verbal inspiration on the part of the inquirer. But observe that none of the narrators claims to give the whole of what Peter said. Observe secondly, that if he said what Matthew records he must have said what the other two record. Observe thirdly, that there is no contradiction in any of the reports. Observe fourthly, that the one feature of his confession which they all record is "the Christ," i. e., the One promised to Israel in the Old Testament prophets, a title which includes all the rest which can be said of Him. And observe finally, that this was the means employed by the Holy Spirit (who inspired the record in every case), to emphasize that one particular feature which He desired to emphasize in coming generations. This goes to substantiate verbal inspiration rather than to weaken it.

A second objection to the mind of the correspondent is found in Acts 5:36, where Luke is assumed to have been mistaken in naming the insurrectionist "Theudas," who is not supposed to have come upon the political horizon until twelve years later. Meyer, the German commentator, is quoted as saying, "A proleptic mistake" was here committed by the writer of the Acts. And who is Meyer? A man whose breath is in his nostrils. What right has he to sit in judgment on the holy men of God who "spake as they were moved by the Holy Ghost"? Who told him this was "a proleptic mistake"? It is just such bombastic remarks by inflated human scholars who should have known better, that have driven an untold number of souls on the rocks of infidelity. How much more sensible as well as Christianlike to say that this Theudas was another of that name than the one Josephus refers to at a later date? Theudas was a common name, and there were many insurrections and insurrectionists.

A third objection bears particularly on the fourth Gospel. "The synoptists state that Jesus' characteristic method of teaching was by parable; but the fourth Gospel does not record a single parable. How is this accounted for on the theory that the writer of the fourth Gospel is John?" I answer, first, that the synoptists state no such thing. Up until an advanced period in His ministry Jesus did not adopt the parabolic mode at all. There was a specific reason for His doing it just then as Matthew states (ch. 13). But this does not imply that He confined himself exclusively thereafter to that method, and the facts are directly contrary to such a theory. It should be remembered, too, that the parables were for the unbelieving multitude more than His own disciples. I answer, second, that the fourth Gospel does contain a single parable, and more than one. Look at chapters 10 and 15, for example. I answer, thirdly, that the date and the purpose of John's Gospel fully explain the difference in style between it and the synoptics. It was later than they by a whole generation. They were written largely for unevangelized communities, and this for the Christian church. They were making converts, this was establishing them. There are other comparisons which might be made and which have a bearing upon the subject, but these are enough.

A fourth objection carries us to the consideration of the second Gospel. It is assumed by the writer that Mark was chronologically the first Gospel, on which supposition he desires to know how to account for the fact that it contains no record of the infancy of Jesus, nor of the post-resurrection Christophany to Peter, etc. But what makes him think that Mark's was the earliest Gospel? It is believed by many others that Matthew's was the earliest. And what has the date of the Gospel to do with the omissions referred to? The Holy Spirit is the Author of the four Gospels; may He not have had some reason for leading one human writer to omit some things which another fully recorded?

Here are summed up what is equivalent to a number of inquiries on the nature of modern researches in the Bible lands, and the bearing they have on the historicity and truth of the Bible.

### THE ROSETTA STONE.

The researches spoken of, date from the early part of the nineteenth century, when, at the close of the Napoleonic wars, a French officer discovered a rare stone in connection with engineering operations near Rosetta at the mouth of the Nile. It was a black basalt stone, about three feet by four feet, containing an inscription in three languages, one of which was Greek but the other two unknown. It was shipped to Europe, and remained an enigma for nearly twenty years, until Champollion, a French scholar, discovered in the Greek a key to the unraveling of the mystery of the other two languages. When this was done the world was put in possession of Egyptian hieroglyphics so that it has been possible to read all the inscriptions on the pyramids, obelisks and other monuments, as well as the writings in the libraries of ancient Egypt, and thus there has been revealed to us the history of the civilization of that people, older than Israel by three or four thousand years. These inscriptions and other writings have thrown a flood of light upon the Old Testament allusions to Israel's connection with Egypt, and prove unmistakably the correctness of them.

### CUNEIFORM LANGUAGE.

A little later than the discovery of the Rosetta stone in Egypt, the way was being prepared for other researches in the Mesopotamian valley in Asia. Travelers for a long while had observed bricks in that locality containing curious wedge-shaped letters, the meaning of which they could not understand, but many of which nevertheless were boxed up and sent to the museums of Europe. Subsequently, God was equipping a young English officer, named Henry Rawlinson, connected with the Persian army, to discover the mystery of these wedge-shaped letters very much as the other mystery had been cleared up in connection with the Rosetta stone. Meanwhile, the French consul at Mosul, Mr. Botta, a trained archeologist, had become interested in digging into certain mounds in the neighborhood of what he took to be the former site of Nineveh. The result of these diggings was, that at length the palace of Sargon, an ancient King of Assyria, was discovered and in connection with it a great library of bricks, with the same wedge-shaped inscriptions. Rawlinson having now mastered this mysterious cuneiform language, as it is called, was able to set before the scholars of the world the mysteries of ancient Assyria and Chaldea just as had formerly been done in the case of Egypt.

### ANCIENT CIVILIZATION.

It was found, for example, that these old nations existed in a highly civilized state thousands of years before the time of Moses, and possessed records of creation substantially the same as those now found in the first and second chapters of Genesis, suggesting that they were obtained from the same source, and that a divine source. The same thing was true of the story of the fall, for while this is not recorded in so many words on any of the monuments, yet it is nevertheless recorded in pictures which leave no mistake upon the mind as to what is intended, for there is seen the tree, the man and the woman, and the serpent in such relationships as to portray the story of the temptation. The deluge also is recorded. The monuments speak of the flood, the ship, the saved family, the saved animals, the birds sent out of the ship, the landing on the mountain, the drying up of the waters and the offering of sacrifice just as in the book of Genesis.

### A Notable Corroboration.

One of the most remarkable corroborations of the record in Genesis was that of the genealogical table in chapter 10. This is now seen to be not a list of names of individuals so much as of nations, and, if true, it is the most valuable ethnographical document in the world, but the discoverers referred to are demonstrating beyond a question that it is absolutely correct as a statement of the origin and dispersion of the nations in every particular. Baron Bunsen, as late as 1854, declared that the statement in that chapter of the Ethiopian origin of Nimrod was only an imagination, but four years afterward, Sir Henry Rawlinson, the decipherer of the cuneiform inscriptions, proved unmistakably that the baron was wrong and the Bible right. Even the tower of Babel has been discovered, and a writing of Nebuchadnezzar has come to light in which he testifies to having rebuilt that tower on its original foundations, the ruins of which are now identified at Birs-Nimroud. Many people have been inclined to laugh at the Biblical record of Abraham and the patriarchs and to relegate it to the realm of myth or allegory, but the whole thing has proven historic; documents written by contemporaries of Abraham in Ur of the Chaldeas have been unearthed, the very names of the kings with whom Abraham did battle, as recorded in Genesis 14, have come to light, and Melchizedek himself is no longer the mysterious person he once was. In the same manner the researches go along side by side with the whole history of Israel down to the close of the Old Testament.

### What is meant by the "synthetic" study of the Bible?

By the "synthetic" study of the Bible is meant the study of the Bible as a whole, and each book of the Bible as a whole, and as seen in its relation to the other books. For a completer and more satisfactory answer the reader is referred to the author's *How to Master the English Bible*. But here it may be said that in the application of the plan, you want to begin at Genesis, for about the same reason you would begin any other book at its beginning, if you really wished to master it. You should read Genesis, if it be possible, right through at a single reading, without observing the arbitrary divisions into chapters and verses. Laying aside the book for the next early opportunity, read it through again in the same way, and again and again, as often as may be necessary, until you have gotten a clear outline of its great outstanding facts in your mind. All this time I would not consult any commentary or other "help" upon that book, and I would resist every temptation or desire to be side-tracked by inquiries into the meaning of this or that detail in the book.

Commentaries and helps have their place, but it is after you have gotten your own possession of the great outline of the book and not before. A comparison of your own outline with that of some distinguished scholar afterwards will probably surprise you as to your own accuracy, a circumstance in itself of no small value to you in your further work, giving courage and confidence to personal research.

After you have done this for Genesis, but not before, approach Exodus in the same way, and then Leviticus, and so on. Some books of the Bible will lend themselves to this method easier than others, and there are two or three, like the Psalms, Proverbs, etc., which need to be approached differently, or which, rather, do not need this kind of approach; but for the most part this is the way to deal with each book in its turn.

There will be some books, like Leviticus and several of the prophets, which will be full of mystery, and tax your patience very much in the matter of waiting to obtain a satisfactory outline for yourself before peeping at the outline of another, but perseverance will yield a rich and lasting reward. You will find, for example, among many other delightful surprises, that as you proceed in your "synthetic" study of the Bible many of the questions and problems confronting you at the first are gradually answering and solving themselves, for the Bible is wondrously self-interpretive, if it be but given an opportunity to be heard.

You may think at first that such a method of studying the Bible is slow and tedious. Slow it may be, but tedious never. The Bible is the most interesting and absorbing book in the world, if properly read; and naturally so, because it has the most interesting Author. Who so interesting a being as God?

As to the time required for its study in this fashion, remember that if it took sixteen hundred years to write it, it should occasion no surprise if it were to take a year or two to understand it. And moreover, the value of giving so much time to its consideration is seen not only in its blessing to us at the present time, but in the time to come. The Bible is the only book in your library which you will carry with you or have any use for in the world to come. Inasmuch as it is a revelation of God as well as a revelation from God, we shall have need of its contents forever. Let us therefore store them up while we can.

Of course, the "synthetic" method of Bible study having accomplished its end when the whole Bible is thus mastered in outline, and each book is seen in its relation to the other books, there are other methods of Bible study to follow, but for those who want to be masters of the English Bible, and able to utilize other methods to the best advantage, this is the way to begin. A rider who learns how to ride a trotting-horse can ride any gaited animal whose back he mounts. Having mastered that gait, he easily adjusts himself to any of the others. But if he has begun with a horse that only canters or single-foots, he is not a rider and never will be, till he learns the foundation gait of all. Get the whole Bible in your mind first in one grand broad view, see it in its dispensational relations, and then you can study it by chapters, or by topics or in any other way to your heart's content, and with increasing profit to yourself and others. Begin any other way, and you will live and die wishing you had begun the right way.

After penning the above, I was pleased to find the following endorsement of the method it urges from so eminent a Bible student and teacher as Rev. F. B. Meyer, of London. After referring to his own habit of spending from half an hour to an hour in the examination of all the passages cognate to some three or four verses, he adds:

"At the same time I can see that if all were to adopt this method they might become so occupied with the hedgerows and the copses of the landscape as to lose the conception of the whole sweep and extent of the panorama of truth. So the extensive must be combined with the intensive, the wider outlook on Scripture as a whole with the microscopic examination of three or four verses." And later on he recurs to the subject of the wider outlook again, the "synthetic" method, and says: "Such should be the plan of Bible study adopted by the young student (the beginner) especially."

I may add, too, that Prof. R. G. Moulton, author of *The Literary Study of the Bible*, and editor of *The English Bible for Modern Readers*, insists upon the same method for the results in Bible study which his valuable work represents.

**The foregoing section on the "synthetic" study of the Bible suggests a further reference to other methods of study.**

One method adopted by some and found interesting and useful is

### THE CHAPTER SUMMARY METHOD.

By this plan the reader goes entirely through the Bible from beginning to end, looking at each chapter carefully in order to discover four things, viz.: (1) the principal subject in each chapter, (2) the leading lesson, (3) the best verse, and (4) the prominent persons named. The Moody Bible Institute of Chicago, makes much of this method.

Another plan known as

### The Topical Method

has been found very helpful in the preparation of prayer meeting talks, Bible readings, etc. Here considerable assistance can be gotten from a good concordance,—Cruden's unabridged, for example—*The Treasury of Scripture Knowledge* or the *Topical Text Book*. The two last-named books are very helpful indeed. *The Treasury of Scripture Knowledge* is really a treasury of marginal references enabling one to do to the best advantage that which Dr. Meyer speaks of as his method, examining cognate passages to see what the Bible has to say in different portions of it on one theme or topic. *The Topical Text Book* is associated with the name of Dr. R. A. Torrey, who has written an introduction for it, and it undertakes to group together under separate heads all the topics whatsoever of which the Scripture chiefly treats, giving the places where the references thereto may be found. It can be seen at once how such a scheme contributes to the thorough study of a particular subject, and lightens the labor of preparing an address upon it.

But no method of Bible study is of avail in the best and truest sense which is carried on independently of the constant and conscious recognition of the need of the Holy Spirit for its exercise. The whole of the second chapter of 1 Corinthians is intended to emphasize that truth, and I entreat its perusal. The Holy Spirit is, in the last analysis, the Author of the Bible (2 Peter 1:21), and everybody will admit that no one is so well equipped to awaken an interest in a book, and illuminate its pages to the understanding as he who wrote it. Moreover, the Holy Spirit dwells in every believer in Christ to do this very thing, "guide us into all truth" (John 16:13); how important, therefore, that we come to know Him as our teacher, supplicating His aid at every step of the way, and expecting that through grace it shall certainly be received! This is the real secret of successful Bible study.

Outside of the knowledge of the essentials of the Christian faith, should you say that all Christians were alike endowed by the Spirit for an understanding of the Word, or are some especially gifted in its study and comprehension?

In Paul's letter to the Colossians (1:28), he speaks of "teaching every man in all (every) wisdom," that he "may present every man perfect in Christ Jesus." This seems to touch upon more than simply "the essentials of the Christian faith," and looks towards the acquirement on the part of all men of a knowledge of "the deep things of God." Moreover, we are exhorted to add to our faith "knowledge." "Grace and peace" are to be "multiplied" unto us "through the knowledge of God and of Jesus our Lord." "All things that pertain unto life and godliness" are said to be given unto us through the same knowledge. This does not look, therefore, as though an aristocracy of the Word were contemplated in the divine counsels. It is a startling thought that the profound teachings of Paul's epistles were addressed to believers, a large majority of whom were but recently escaped from heathenism, and that these included children who are addressed directly and not through their parents. Here are considerations for deep and earnest inquiry on our part.

It is indeed true that Paul speaks in 1 Corinthians 12, of some who had the gift of "knowledge"; but in the same connection he exhorts us to "covet earnestly the best gifts." Who can doubt that the earnest coveting of a knowledge of God's Word on the part of any one would result in the possession of that gift? It is like what Dr. A. B. Simpson would say of divine healing, viz.: "It is quite right to ask God to bless the best means we know, if we do not know a better way." In other words, he thinks that all Christians may have the faith to be healed supernaturally, if they will. Certainly I think all Christians may have a like deep and broad understanding of the Word, if they will. It may not please God to give all His servants the like gift of teaching the Word, because there is necessity for the exercise of other gifts, but it has never seemed to me that the knowledge of the Word and the teaching of it stood alike in this respect.

**What version of the Bible would you recommend for the "synthetic" study of the Bible, Authorized, Revised, or American Revised?**

My own choice is what is called the *Two-Version Edition*, being the Authorized Version with the differences of the Revised Version printed in the margin, so that both texts can be read from the same page. This has the additional advantage of the alternative readings of the *Revised Version*, and largely does away with the need of the *American Revised*. It is one of the Oxford publications.

To use the *Revised Version* thus as a commentary on the King James is preferable to using the former alone, since very often the two renderings throw different light on the thought of inspiration, aiding materially in its exposition and application. But if I were shut up to an absolute choice between the *King James* and the *Revised*, I should, notwithstanding all its pronounced literary defects, select the former, and I should do this on doctrinal grounds. It is true that the *Revised Version* is in many respects a great improvement on the *King James*, but in certain instances it diverges from the old lines of truth just enough to make its general acceptance in the place of the King James lead to very serious consequences of a rationalistic character. Its rendering of Colossians 1:15, 1 Timothy 3:16 and 2 Timothy 3:16 are in point. Any who desire to examine into the subject further would be interested in reading Dean Bargon's, *The Revision Revised*, or *Remarks on the Revised Version*, by Benjamin Wills Newton, both of which are English publications.

If the *King James Version* is chosen, the most valuable edition of it at this time is the *Scofield Reference Bible*. Indeed every Christian worker should have a copy of it.

## CHAPTER II.

### QUESTIONS ON THE DOCTRINE OF GOD.

Please explain about the voice heard from heaven at the baptism of Jesus. If Christ was God manifested in the flesh, then God was on the earth. Who, under these circumstances, could have spoken from heaven?

God is a Spirit who is omnipresent, that is, present everywhere on earth and in heaven at the same time. He was in heaven even when He was on earth incarnate in Jesus Christ. Moreover, while there is only one God, yet in the Godhead there are three Persons, the Father, Son and Holy Spirit, all three of whom are brought before us at the baptism of Jesus. It was the voice of the Father that was heard from heaven; it was the Son incarnate that was standing in the water, while it was the Holy Spirit who came upon Him in anointing power and whose presence was indicated by the symbolism of the dove. Of course, these things are deeply mysterious and baffle our understanding, but we are to accept them by faith, and square our lives in accordance with them if we would be blest.

**Can an unbeliever in Christ claim God as his Father?**

God is the Father of all men in the sense that He created them, but He is the Father of some men in the sense that He regenerated them. Certainly in this latter sense the unbeliever can not claim Him as his Father.

**Can the doctrine of the universal Fatherhood of God be proved on the strength of such passages as 1 Corinthians 8:6; Ephesians 4:6; John 8:41 and 6:44?**

It can not be proved on the strength of the first two passages named, because the inspired writer is there addressing himself to Christians, i. e., to believers only. He says that God is their Father. Neither can it be proved from the third passage named, because the unbelieving Jews are there making the claim for themselves, which Jesus immediately denies in the next verse. He tells them plainly that God is not their Father. Finally, it can not be proven from the last passage, for Jesus just as plainly says in the verse following that every man who knows the Father will come to Him the Savior, i. e., will believe on Him. As men do not universally do this there can be no claim made of the universal Fatherhood of God.

**Do you understand Paul's teaching on Mars Hill to give countenance to the "liberal" theology on the universal Fatherhood of God and brotherhood of man?**

Certainly not. Paul was dealing with the philosophical Athenians on the natural plane of things, as the context of Acts 17 shows, and on which plane it is true, of course, that God, as Creator, is the Father of us all, and that we, being His offspring, are of one blood, and in that sense, brothers. But the New Testament just as clearly teaches the necessity of a new birth, and that in another sense God becomes the Father of them that believe on His Son Jesus Christ, and that all such believers become "brethren" in Him. We need to be very careful in using that popular phrase lest we fall into the snare of the Devil and teach that all men are in a saved condition, needing no regeneration and no reconciliation to God through the atonement of Jesus Christ. Personally, I seldom use the phrase, because it has become so misleading in the hands of false teachers, and when I do use it I am always careful to explain that I mean that Fatherhood of God and brotherhood of man, which are based upon and grow out of the redemption which is by faith in Christ Jesus.

**Harnack, in his "What Is Christianity?" says, "The Gospel is the knowledge and recognition of God as the**

Father," and that God's Fatherhood is the main article in Jesus' message. Is this true, and what does he mean?

Harnack means that relationship of Father which exists between God and all mankind as their Creator, for he recognizes no other. But when he says that Jesus came to reveal God as Father in this sense he is teaching error. In the first place, there were no need of such a revelation, since even the heathen knew God as Father in this sense. Paul teaches this in his address on Mars Hill, when he quotes from their own poets to prove it. Moreover, the Jews recognized God as Father in this sense, and also in the higher sense as embraced in the Abrahamic covenant.

Therefore, the conception of the Fatherhood of God which Jesus came to reveal was not the universal Fatherhood, not a relationship depending on creation nor yet on the Abrahamic covenant, but on a new birth by the Spirit of God. "That this sonship was strictly limited to those who were thus born again is the plain teaching of the fourth Gospel," says Sir Robert Anderson in his *Christianized Rationalism*, a reply to Dr. Harnack, and he adds, "But no more emphatic denial of the figment of universal Fatherhood in this sphere will be found in the fourth Gospel than is contained in the following words in the first:—"No one knoweth the Son save the Father; neither doth any know the Father save the Son, and he to whomsoever the Son willeth to reveal Him" (Matthew 11:27).

**Does God change the old heart of the believer, or put a new motive beside the old one?**

He gives the believer on Christ a new heart altogether, which means a new will, purpose, motive, spirit, nature—in short, a new life. His own Holy Spirit becomes the possession of the believer, and in the measure in which the latter yields and surrenders himself to God's Holy Spirit is he enabled to live a life of victory over sin of every kind, every day. It will be helpful to read 2 Corinthians 5:17 and Galatians 5:16, 17 (R. V.).

**Please explain the apparently contradictory statements in the Bible where God is sometimes spoken of as "repenting," and sometimes as One who does not "repent," or change His mind.**

The answer is that in these cases the real change is in man and not in God. As Dr. Joseph Parker puts it: "All the government of God is founded upon a moral basis; when moral conditions have been impaired or disturbed, God's relation to the matter in question is of necessity changed; and this change, justified by such reasons, could not be more conveniently expressed than by the word repentance." We thus see, as another expresses it, that it is because God is unchangeable that He is said to repent.

**Why did God punish Pharaoh when He hardened Pharaoh's heart?**

This question is often asked with the hope of finding some flaws in God's character whereby He may be blamed, and man in some sense justified. But it is always a failure. God is true though every man a liar. Nineteen times in Exodus is that word "hardened" used with reference to Pharaoh's heart. Sometimes it is God who is said to do the hardening and sometimes Pharaoh himself, but, to quote *The Mosaic Era* (Gibson), "The two things are really identical. Pharaoh, by his conduct, put himself under the operation of the invariable law, by which a man's heart becomes harder the longer he resists divine mercy and grace. Inasmuch as the law spoken of was God's law, God hardened his heart. It is the same process viewed from its two sides. We must not suppose God singled out Pharaoh, or that He singles out any one, and says, "I will harden his heart." But "by the operation of the law according to which the soul becomes less and less susceptible to impressions which have been resisted, God hardens the heart of every one who does not yield to Him" (*Alleged Discrepancies of the Bible*, Bates). See in this connection, Romans 1:18-23 and 2 Thessalonians 2:8-12.

### How do you harmonize God's command to destroy the Amalekites (1 Samuel 15) with His love, mercy and compassion?

That is always the way with the natural heart. We want to know how to harmonize God's justice, holiness and truth with His "love, mercy and compassion," but we seldom reverse the terms and want to know how to harmonize His "love, mercy and compassion" with His justice, holiness and truth. Instead of wondering why a loving, merciful, and compassionate God destroyed the Amalekites, why not wonder why a just, holy and true God bore with them so long? Why does He bear with any of us? Why especially was He willing to put our sins on the Person of His Son that they who believe on Him might be saved?

Look at the latter half of Exodus 17, and you will learn something about these Amalekites, and read in the same connection 1 Samuel 15:18, and observe the word "sinners." Their cup of iniquity was full. They had sinned again and again, grossly sinned against light, and mercy, and forbearance, and had become permanently fixed in their rebellion and opposition to God. There is an end to God's mercy sometimes; His justice, which is as inherent as His love, demands this; and He could not command the respect of His creatures if this were not so. Moreover, it is necessary to God's righteous judgment of a sinful and rebellious race, that signal and awful illustrations of His judgment upon the incorrigibly wicked should at times be manifested. It is an act of mercy on His part to destroy a few that the many may be warned and some saved. The Scriptures have truly said, "It is a fearful thing to fall into the hands of the living God" (Hebrews 10:31).

### Does God choose some men on the ground of their foreseen capability of good?

God acts sovereignly in election according to grace, and does not choose any man on the ground of "foreseen capability of good." To do this were to make man his own savior in a great degree. See Ephesians 2:8, 9 and Titus 3:4-7.

### How do we know the Holy Spirit is God?

He is called God. In Acts 5:3 Peter accused Ananias of lying to the Holy Ghost; and in the next verse he said that he did not lie to a mere man, but to God. In Jeremiah 31:31-34 we are told that the Lord Jehovah spoke about a new covenant that He would make, while according to Hebrew 10:15-17 it was the Holy Ghost who thus spake. See 2 Corinthians 3:17.

### What are some of the best works on the Holy Spirit?

One of the fullest and richest books is quite an old one, that entitled, *On the Holy Spirit*, by John Owen, in two volumes. It was written in 1674, but a more recent edition has been published, copies of which may be found in the second-hand bookstores. While the style is heavy and involved after the manner of the Puritans, yet the richness of the mine will repay the cost of the digging. It is from this source that many, if not most, of the later English writers on the subject have drawn most extensively. Another book, highly recommended just now, is by the Dutch theologian, Abraham Kuyper, entitled *The Work of the Holy Spirit*. It is an encyclopedia of inspiration and discussion on the subject. Among smaller and less expensive books, I would name first, *Through the Eternal Spirit*, by the Scotch divine, James Elder Cumming. If you can only get one, get this. Then come *Lectures on the Doctrine of the Holy Spirit*, by William Kelly; *The Ministry of the Spirit*, by A. J. Gordon; *The Spirit of Christ*, by Andrew Murray; *The Tongue of Fire*, by William Arthur; *The Acts of the Holy Spirit*, by A. T. Pierson; *The Spirit-Filled Life*, by John MacNeil; and *Plain Papers on the Holy Spirit*, by C. I. Scofield.

# CHAPTER III.

## QUESTIONS ON THE PERSON OF CHRIST.

**Why give the date of the nativity as B. C. 4, instead of A. D. 1?**

The date of the nativity is calculated in its relation to the date of the founding of the city of Rome. For a time it was supposed to have occurred in the 754th year of that city, making the Christian era, or, as we say, A. D., begin at that time. But more recently scholars have come to the conclusion that a mistake was made in the original calculation. One of the data was the period of the reign of Herod the Great, and investigation has shown this to be four years earlier than it was hitherto supposed. The earlier date for Herod carries with it the earlier date for the birth of Christ, which must have been, not in the 754th year of Rome, but the 750th. This is still, therefore, A. D. 1913, only the years must be reckoned not from what has usually been called A. D. 1, or the year of Rome 754, but B. C. 4, or the year of Rome 750. There is no practical difference, as the inquirer will see, but if one is to speak with chronological exactness the Christian era began four years earlier than is popularly supposed, judging by the chronology of Rome.

**Under what "law" was it that Christ was made (or born), and why?**

The law here is the whole of the moral and ceremonial law of Moses. Christ was made under that law in the sense that, as a Jew, He was born subject to it. But furthermore, He was made under it by His Father's appointment and His own free will, to keep it as our representative and substitute, and to suffer and exhaust the full penalty of our violation of it. "This," to quote the *Bible Commentary*, "constitutes the significance of His circumcision, His presentation in the temple, His baptism by John, and other circumstances and events in His earthly life." He came into the world thus to "fulfill all righteousness."

### Please explain Isaiah 7:14-16.

The prophet may be speaking of some maiden in Judah, (perhaps about to become his wife), that would become married and give birth to a son in the natural way, who should be called by the name mentioned, "Immanuel." And before this son should arrive at an age of moral consciousness, just a few years evidently from the time when the prophet was speaking, the enemies that the king was fearing so greatly would be overcome by God's power. This "sign" of God's goodness to him and to the nation was offered to the king for his encouragement and guidance if he were willing to receive it.

But while this is the historical setting of the prophecy, the Holy Spirit uses it, as we see from Matthew 1:23, as applicable in a higher sense to the birth of our Lord and Savior Jesus Christ. This is in accordance with a "law of double reference" frequently employed in the Word of God, by which two events are blended in one, having a near and partial, and also a remote and complete fulfillment.

### Please explain the word "compass" as found in Jeremiah 31:22.

Although this question at first seems far enough away from the preceding one just answered, yet it really relates to the same thing—Jesus, the seed of Abraham.

In this chapter the prophet is speaking of Israel's backsliding and sin which was about to be punished by their Babylonian captivity; and he is exhorting them to repent and return to God. He encourages them to do this by the wonderful promise that "Jehovah hath created (is about to create) a new thing in the earth, a woman shall compass a man." The reference is to the forthcoming incarnation of the Son of God, the Virgin birth of Jesus. He was encompassed by supernatural power in the womb of Mary. There are several reasons leading to this application of the words, one or two of which appear in the text itself. For example, the word "created" implies a divine power put forth in the creation of the body in the virgin's womb by the Holy Spirit (Luke 1:35; Hebrews 10:5). The phrase, "a new thing" also, means something unprecedented; it means a man whose like had never existed before, and a mother out of the ordinary course of nature, at once a mother and a virgin. Finally, the Hebrew for "man," in this instance, is properly translated "mighty man," a term sometimes applied to God as in Deuteronomy 10:17, and to Christ in Zechariah 13:7 (*Bible Commentary*).

### Did our Savior have any help from God before He was twelve years of age that other children do not have?

It is to be remembered that Jesus differed from all other children in that He was born without sin. See Hebrews 4:15 and 7:26. In this respect He resembled Adam before the fall. That is not to say that He was not subject to temptation like other boys, or that He might not have fallen, but He did not have the inward propensity to yield that they have. In the same connection, however, it should be stated that any boy who will yield himself to God will receive the fulness of the Spirit of Jesus by which he will be enabled to follow in His footsteps; and while he never will become like his Savior, sinless, yet he will have power to resist the tempter, and live a life of victory over every known sin.

### Was Christ dipped clear under the water at the time of His baptism?

If this question could be answered positively one way or the other, it would contribute more than any other fact to settle the vexed question of the mode of baptism which has troubled the church for centuries. There are those who strongly insist that He was put under the water, but there are scholars on the other side, just as devout, who can not see it that way, and every man must be fully persuaded in his own mind.

**Was it for the sake of others only, or for His own sake as well, that Jesus was tempted?**

My judgment is, that it was for His own sake, and for that of His people also. The subject is of the profoundest character, and we should be careful not to be wise above what is written; but the temptation seems to have been a girding of Jesus for His ministry, a necessary test and discipline, considering Him now as a man only, by means of which He was further approved and qualified for His work. At the same time His victory was a victory for us, not merely in its moral example, but in its substitutionary effect on the power of Satan as our tempter. His strength being broken, the believer on Jesus has now only to resist him and he will flee from him (James 4:7).

**Did Jesus know beforehand of the transfiguration experience?**

How long beforehand He may have known one can hardly answer, but that He had some pre-intimation of it is evident from the context of the story, since He promised a foregleam of His glory to His disciples about six days before it transpired.

**Is there any sense in which it may be said that Jesus had power to save Himself from the cross had He chosen to exercise it?**

The reference is to Jesus considered as to His human nature. The question is a "deep" one, indeed, and yet I apprehend that much of the moral value of the sufferings of the cross depends upon their voluntariness. The twelfth chapter of John seems to contain an intimation that

Jesus might have saved Himself from the cross, "but for this cause came I unto this hour." Had He possessed such a desire and yielded to it, what would have become of this poor lost world? would it not have remained in that condition? And what about the personal glory of Jesus Himself considered as a man? would it not have been forfeited? For the "joy that was set before Him He endured the cross, despising the shame." But suppose the cross had not been endured, would the joy have followed?

**How many contemporaneous writers make mention of the Lord Jesus and of His resurrection?**

Lardner, in his *Collection of Ancient Jewish and Heathen Testimonies to the Truth of the Christian Religion*, quotes about seventy writers of the first six centuries who used their pens against Christ and His cause. These often admit the authenticity of the Gospels and their accuracy with reference to persons, places and events, including the resurrection, but in many instances try to explain away the miraculous on other grounds.

**How do you harmonize Matthew 28:1; Mark 16:1; Luke 24:1 and John 20:1, which refer to the events of the resurrection morning?**

Luke says it was the first day of the week very early in the morning; John says when it was yet dark; Matthew, as it began to dawn; Mark says that though it was very early when they left home, they came to the sepulchre at the rising of the sun. In that latitude the interval between the dawn and the morning is very brief.

John names only Mary Magdalene, who, when she saw the sepulchre, ran to meet Peter and John, saying, "We know not where they have laid Him." The plural "we" shows that there must have been more women with her though only she is mentioned by this evangelist. Matthew speaks of her and the other Mary. Mark speaks of her and Mary the mother of James and Salome. Luke tells of the same two, adds the name of Johanna, and mentions "other women." There is no contradiction here. Neither is there any in the reference to the angels, or the actions of the women or the other disciples. A little patient thinking, and a little common sense, will unravel a great many so-called "discrepancies" in the Bible.

**How was Christ in the earth three days and three nights, if He was buried on Friday and rose the first day of the week?**

Some would say he was buried on Thursday, and a strong argument can be presented for this view, but the common interpretation is, that the "three days and three nights" are to be interpreted according to the Jewish custom of accounting a part of a day as a whole day. Christ was in the earth parts of Friday, Saturday and Sunday, and this, according to the custom aforementioned, was "three days and three nights."

**Where was the soul of Jesus during the three days His body lay in the grave (Luke 23:43; John 20:17; Acts 2:27)?**

In the first Scripture passage referred to, Jesus speaks of being that day in Paradise; in the second, He declares (after His resurrection) that He had not yet ascended to the Father and in the third, speaking through the prophet David, He declares His soul was not left in "hell," or as it should be translated, "hades." Hades is a Greek word signifying the abode of the dead, not necessarily the wicked dead any more than the righteous dead, but the dead generically speaking. The Jews of the time of Christ regarded it as comprised of two compartments as it were, one for the righteous, and the other for the wicked dead. The first-named, the place of the righteous dead in hades, is thought to be synonymous with the Paradise spoken of in Luke. Of course, this is not the abode of the Father to which He had not yet ascended. For further considerations of this subject the correspondent is referred to the author's *Progress in the Life to Come*.

### Is Jesus' body now the same as that in which He arose from the dead?

As to the present body of Jesus Christ, there is no Scriptural proof that I recall to indicate whether it is now the same as that in which He arose from the dead, or whether it was changed at the time of His ascension. The peculiarity of His body during the forty days intervening between His resurrection and ascension would not seem to call for any essential change after the last event; while we do not forget the testimony of the angels to the disciples on Mount Olivet (Acts 1:11), "This same Jesus, which was taken up from you into heaven, shall so come in like manner as He was seen to go into heaven."

### What is the relation of the ascension of Christ to the Christian believer?

The doctrine of the Ascension of Christ is not dwelt upon with the frequency and attention its importance in the Christian scheme deserves. The incarnation, death and resurrection of Christ are each and all of them, seriously and vitally incomplete without the ascension, just as that event itself awaits the fruition of its purpose in a return of the ascended Lord in glory to the earth.

But that which gives peculiar interest to the ascension is its active bearing upon our spiritual life today. We are redeemed by the death and resurrection of Christ considered as a single act, but that is past. We are to be raised from the dead ourselves, and glorified at His second coming, but that is future. We are being saved, established in the faith, enlightened in the knowledge of God, sanctified, anointed and equipped for service, and that is going on at present, and as the result of our Savior's presence as our High Priest at the right hand of God.

### Will you explain Hebrews 9:12-23 with special reference to the question whether Christ literally took His material blood with Him to heaven?

Light will be thrown on the passage by a comparison of the Revised Version, which, at verse 12, reads, "through His own blood entered in once for all." The meaning seems to be that by virtue of His shed blood He entered there. It is written in the Scripture that "the life is in the blood," and the general belief is that Christ's life in heaven as our once sacrificed Savior but now risen and interceding High Priest is what is meant by the verses under consideration. I am not aware of any commentator who takes the view that He presents His material blood in the holy place.

### Will you explain the relation of Jehovah of the Old Testament to Jesus of the New?

1. "Jehovah" is one of the names of the Triune God, and is in that sense the name of God the Father, the Son, and the Holy Ghost. Now that Person of the Godhead who has appeared to men is the Second Person only. It was He who appeared to Moses at the burning bush, to Abraham on the plains of Mamre and the other patriarchs; and it was He who became incarnate in Jesus Christ.

2. As to the "appearances" of Jehovah to Abraham, Genesis 12:7; 17:1; 18:1, the correspondent would like to know if they were visible to Abraham's physical eyes, or seen only in a vision? The last-named certainly was a visible representation, and while the same is not stated with reference to the two preceding ones, it would be rather hazardous, perhaps, to say that they were otherwise. And yet to regard them as visions may not be to take too great liberty with the Word of God.

3. As to "the Angel of the Lord," Genesis 16:7, and "the Angel of God," Genesis 21:17, I think there is no difference. This is another of the titles of Jehovah himself, always representing the Second Person of the Trinity.

### Is the "Name above every name" in Philippians 2:9, one yet to be given to Christ?

No, the grammar of the verses indicates that it has already

been given to Him. It is the Name of "Jesus" mentioned in the next verse, "which," as another says, "is even now in glory his Name of honor." We now worship in the Name of Jesus which proves it to be above every name. Moreover, "Whosoever shall call upon the 'Name' of the Lord shall be saved,"—how this exalts that precious Name! Many more such Scriptural allusions will be recalled.

In the same connection the writer asks whether the name "Jehovah" as used in the Old Testament always refers to Jesus?

I think not, except, of course, in the sense that it is the name of God, and Jesus, as to His divine nature, is God. But wherever "Jehovah" is spoken of in the Old Testament as manifesting Himself to men there, I think, the Second Person of the Trinity is designated. With this understanding of the subject it is proper to say, that the Jesus of the New Testament is the Jehovah of the Old.

# CHAPTER IV.

## QUESTIONS ON THE CHURCH.

**If the church is the body of Christ, as we are taught in Ephesians and Colossians, how can she be at the same time His bride?**

The inconsistency of the church being the body and the bride in one is lessened by the analogy of Adam and Eve. She was his bride, but a part of his body too. She was his body also before she was his bride. As to the time and place of the marriage of the glorified Bridegroom and the bride, I suppose it will be at the rapture when the church is caught up to meet the Lord in the air (1 Thessalonians 4:13-18).

**Is the kingdom of heaven the same as the church, and if not, what is meant by that phrase?**

The "kingdom of heaven" in the New Testament, is not synonymous with the church, although I doubt not it includes the church. It includes also Israel in the flesh, restored to her own land, penitent, converted to Jesus as her Messiah and the governmental head of the nations on the earth during the millennium. The church at this time will be with her Head, Jesus Christ, in a glorified state in the heavenly places in the air, as Paul states in 1 Thessalonians 4; and these two divisions, if we may so speak of them, restored Israel and the glorified church, constitute together what I understand by the "kingdom of heaven." The Sermon on the Mount, of which the inquirer speaks, is rather to be regarded as the "constitution," or rules for the earthly division of the kingdom, i. e., Israel in the flesh, than for the church or heavenly seat of the kingdom. The prayer, "Thy kingdom come," was certainly not answered on the Day of Pentecost.

except in an initial sense, or as one step in the direction of its complete answer as indicated above. It is still proper to offer that prayer until the consummation alluded to is realized.

**What is the meaning of 2 Corinthians 6:14, and does it teach that one should withdraw from the church under such circumstances?**

When Paul urges believers to have no fellowship with unbelievers, he can not mean that the former "should leave the church," for, if so, where would they go? Believers do themselves constitute the church, and wherever they are assembled there the church is assembled. He means that believers should not mingle with the world. They should not marry the world's people (1 Corinthians 7:39, last clause), nor should they worship the world's gods (1 Corinthians 10:16-23). If unbelievers are in the visible church as the correspondent states, they should not be there, and it is a sinful "fellowship" that admits them.

**How do you explain Christ's charge to Peter in Matthew 16:18, and the related passage, John 20:23?**

The passages do not mean that Peter was the first pope. It is fatal to the theory of the papacy that Peter never really visited Rome. His name means "rock," indeed, but the rock on which the church is built is not Peter himself, but the confession of Christ which Peter had just made. This is suggested in the first verse referred to, where the words translated "Peter" in one case, and "rock" in the other, are in different genders, signifying in the first instance a small stone, and in the next, a great rock. Moreover, the allusion to "the keys" in the next verse is qualified by the reference to John where we find the authority thus given to Peter was extended to the rest of the twelve disciples.

Just what that authority was, the binding and loosing, is further explained by Matthew 18:18, in the light of its context. It seems to have been the power of discipline delegated to the twelve disciples at the first, but through them to the whole church afterwards. The reception of members into the church, or the excommunication of the heretical and unruly by the whole body acting as such, comes as near to the interpretation and application of these words as anything I know. There is, however, a further and particular application of "the keys" in Peter's case, as seen in the fact that he was privileged to first preach the Gospel to the Jews on the Day of Pentecost (Acts 2), and to the Gentiles of the household of the centurion (Acts 10, 11), thus opening the kingdom of heaven to the two great classes of men.

### Why do not men go to church? Is the church at fault?

Fundamentally, men do not go to church because of the sinful condition of the natural heart, which lacks the taste for divine things. But in a secondary sense, the church is in some instances open to blame. The strongest attraction the church can offer, even to men of the world, is a wholesome spiritual service where the reading and exposition of the Word of God is the prime feature; but this is an attraction not as generally employed as it should be. It is a mistake to suppose that men like to hear ministers discuss social, economical and political affairs in the pulpit, except in rare instances. Such themes are better treated in other places, and men are surfeited with them six days in the week. The Word of God, however, properly handled, is always fresh and freshening.

But after all, why should the church be so insistent that men come to her? Was not the command for her to go to them? Open-air preaching for half the year is the secret of reaching men in many communities. When they get a taste of the Gospel in the streets they like to listen to it again within church walls. Many pastors both in this and the old country are adopting the plan of preaching on their church steps once or twice a week besides Sundays, and it works splendidly. Try it.

**How can you explain Paul's views concerning woman?**

In the first place, they are not "Paul's views." They are the commandments of God spoken by the lips, or rather written by the hand of Paul. All Scripture is given by inspiration of God (2 Timothy 3:16). Paul himself says, "Which things we speak, not in the words which man's wisdom teacheth, but which the Holy Ghost teacheth" (1 Corinthians 2:13).

In 1 Corinthians 11:5, Paul, by the Spirit of God, permits a woman to pray or prophesy in the church, providing it is done with that becoming modesty as to apparel and demeanor which the canons of the time and place set forth. "Prophesying" here does not mean simply the foretelling of events, but such speaking as generally goes by the name of preaching or exhorting—just such speaking as we hear, or should hear, in our church prayer meetings.

But in the same epistle, chapter 14:34, 35, Paul commands that "women keep silence in the churches," a command repeated in 1 Timothy 2:11. Whatever it may mean in these instances, clearly its meaning cannot be made to contradict what is just permitted in 1 Corinthians 11:5.

To look first at 1 Corinthians 14:34,35. The injunction to silence is mentioned three times in that chapter, verses 28, 30 and 34, twice with reference to men, and once with reference to women, and in every case it is conditional and not absolute. He who speaks in an unknown tongue is to keep silence if there be no interpreter. He who has a revelation is to keep silence if there be a revelation given to another sitting by. In like manner the women are to keep silence if their questions interrupt the order and decorum of the service. Throughout the whole chapter the apostle is dealing with the various causes of disorder and confusion in the conduct of the public worship of the church, and is not to be interpreted as if he were repressing the proper exercise of spiritual gifts by either sex. So says A. J. Gordon, in a careful treatment of this subject, and so am I inclined to believe. If Paul were forbidding women to take part in prayer and prophesying in public religious meetings, "What," as Dr. Gordon says, "could be more irrelevant or meaningless than the command, 'If they will learn anything, let them ask their husbands at home'?" The apostle should have said, if they will pray or prophesy to the edification of any one let it be to their husbands at home. Dr. Jacobs, in his *Ecclesiastical Polity*, a very valuable work of its kind, takes the same view.

Turning now to 1 Timothy 2, let us read the context from verse 8. The apostle is exhorting men to pray everywhere in a certain fashion and spirit, and at verse 9 he does the same to women. Many commentators feel that the "I will" of verse 8 is to be carried over to verse 9, making the latter read in this way: "In like manner, I will that women pray in modest apparel," etc.

In verses 11 and 12, however, the apostle is passing on to something else, viz.: the relation of the married woman to her husband. She is to learn rather than to teach, to be in subjection to him rather than have authority over him. The author already alluded to quotes Canon Garrett in his work, *The Ministry of Women*, as sustaining this view. Another commentator, reasoning back from verse 12 to those before, thinks women may have been enjoined from public teaching as distinguished from public praying and prophesying. The work of teacher and pastor are about identical, and there is no record in the Scripture of a woman being placed in such authority over a church.

## Do you understand that Christ commanded the washing of the disciples' feet as an ordinance similar to the Lord's Supper?

I do not understand that Christ commanded washing the disciples' feet "as an ordinance similar to the Lord's Supper," and I know of no record in the New Testament showing that it was so observed in the apostolic church.

The history and significance of the incident as given in John 13 seems to be like this: Feet-washing under such circumstances serves in the East, not as a religious ordinance, but a social custom. Men wore sandals, not shoes, and of necessity their feet were soiled in traveling. When entering a house as guests, water and a towel were always provided for their accommodation, as well as a servant to perform the office. If the host wished to show special honor to his guest he would perform the office in his own person.

In the present instance, Jesus was the host and His disciples the guests; and the lesson He taught on the surface was that so beautifully emphasized afterwards by Peter on whom this circumstance made so profound an impression. See 1 Peter 5:5, especially in the Revised Version. It was not so much that they should wash one another's feet but that they should be ever ready to serve one another with humility, not excluding even the washing of feet, when occasion called.

Almost every expositor who has dealt particularly with that chapter, however, has seen something deeper in that action of Christ than the physical washing of His disciples' feet. They have regarded it as a type of His high-priestly function as intercessor, and if so, the corresponding service we disciples are to render one another is interceding for one another, and the putting away of one another's sin as indicated in Galatians 6:1-3 and James 5:16, 19, 20.

I see no harm in the observance of the literal washing of the feet as an ordinance, and can understand how the symbol might be made very useful in emphasizing the obligation symbolized, but that is not to say that I regard it as a divinely instituted ordinance.

**What is the objection to raising money for church support by means of fairs, socials, etc.?**

There is quite a difference in these things and in Christian opinion concerning them. There seems to be no objection to ladies doing sewing, embroidery work, making cake and delicacies, and selling the product of their labor at a fair price for the benefit of the Lord's work. But the average church fair is not usually content with such prosaic features. Things frivolous, worldly and sensational are often introduced. Storekeepers, under pressure, are made to contribute articles, and visitors, in the same way, are made to buy them. All this lowers the dignity of the Christian religion and cultivates false standards of Christian giving.

**What is the objection to holding these affairs in the church building?**

There is no objection in the abstract. If it is right to hold them at all, it can hardly be wrong, according to Protestant ideas of sacred places, to hold them anywhere that may be found convenient. And yet even the most pronounced iconoclasts as to churchly venerations dislike to see and hear the concomitants of a bazaar in the same room where they are accustomed to meet to worship God in other ways and at other times.

**Are there any Scriptural passages in opposition to gymnasiums, reading rooms, and other institutional features in connection with a church building?**

No, the inspired Word does not go into details of that kind, but rather lays down the great principles of church government. It is certainly in harmony with the spirit of Christianity to provide for the physical, mental and social betterment of the race, but whether such enterprises should be carried on under the direction of the church organization, and beneath the same roof is a question with very many. Their care and especially their proximity would seem to detract from the real objective of the church which is spiritual and evangelistic. My own idea is that Christian men and women should be interested in these things, but that they should be separated organically from the church. However, there are exceptions to every rule, and in a small town circumstances may dictate a different course. "If any of you lack wisdom, let him ask of God, that giveth to all men liberally, and upbraideth not" (James 1:5).

A correspondent makes certain statements and asks certain questions about the church and denominationalism, which will be sufficiently understood in the replies that follow:

For example, he is right in supposing that the church in a spiritual sense, or considered as the body of which Christ is the head, is composed of all those individuals, and only of those, who are united to Him by a living, personal faith; and, I may add, a faith wrought in them by the power of the Holy Spirit.

Also, is he right in supposing that the local church or congregation of Christians, is a number of such believers regularly meeting together in any one place for the worship of God and the administration of the sacraments without reference to any particular denominational name by which they may be called.

But I think he is wrong in supposing that "denominationalism is a device of the Devil to divide God's people." There are aspects of and features in denominationalism which may sometimes suggest that idea to some people, but, on the other hand, denominationalism is almost a necessity in the present age. Take the denominational lines indicated by the division into Calvinists and Arminians, for example. The apparently opposite positions for which these schools of religious thought stand are both found in the Bible, viz.: God's sovereignty and man's free agency; but it would seem as though no one finite mind could hold both equally at the same time. How necessary, however, that both be duly emphasized! The Calvinist is necessary to the Arminian, and *vice versa*.

Take the question of baptism, its mode and its subjects, which is another line of denominational cleavage. I feel convinced that that important subject is kept alive amongst us by the very controversy occasioned by this difference of opinion.

The matter of church government divides again, and the necessity to defend independence against prelacy, or one order in the ministry against two or three, compels the whole question of church order or rule to keep to the fore as it ought to do.

Then there are other good features of denominationalism, for example, the zeal created by a proper and just rivalry in the work of the Lord, especially in missions. I am aware that denominationalism works ill on the foreign field, but it works good, too, and doubtless the good far outweighs the ill. Of course, I am speaking now of conditions as they are. In a holier and more enlightened age denominations will not have a place, and will not be required, but for the present we are hardly justified in describing them as unqualifiedly of the devil.

**The laboring men in the community where I live feel that the church is opposed to their interests. How can we harmonize the two elements? What is the best method of paving the way for presenting the Gospel message to the laboring men?**

The church is not opposed to the laboring men and their interests, but the very opposite. Therefore, the course to pursue in the circumstances, is to show what the true church is, viz., the body of Christ in which He lives, and through which He now manifests Himself on earth. This means that we must be always faithful to the Gospel and the Word of God in our teaching and preaching, never losing sight of the fact that men are lost and need salvation before all things.

If in our zeal to harmonize the laboring man and the church we deviate into lines of social service, we are making a mistake the result of which will be the widening of the gulf in the end. That is not to say that, as individual

Christians, we should not show an interest in the social needs of the laboring man, and do what we can for their betterment, but only that as representatives of the Gospel of Jesus Christ we should not allow its meaning to be confused by accentuating side issues.

The best method of "paving the way" for presenting the Gospel message to laboring men is to present the message, which will amply take care of itself when presented in the power of the Holy Spirit.

**Do you approve of the Passion Play? And what is your opinion of the display of its pictures with a lecture at a church service?**

I have never seen the Passion Play and only know of it as I have read descriptions and seen pictures of it in public print. But personally, I would not go to see it, no matter how convenient it might be, esteeming it sacrilegious. This is not to say that emotions may not be stirred by it which some people would esteem holy; neither is it to criticize my fellow Christians who endorse the play, but simply to answer the question as intelligently and conscientiously as I can.

I feel about the play as I do about a portrait or image of Jesus Christ. I would not dishonor our Lord by possessing one or having one on my premises, no matter how superior the artist who produced it.

The thought that a sinful man, and all men are sinful, could produce a picture of a holy man, seems absurd; and when we consider who the holy man in question is, it approaches blasphemy, to my mind.

## CHAPTER V.

### QUESTIONS ON THE CHRISTIAN MINISTRY.

**How many orders are there in the Christian ministry?**

There were apparently two offices in the church to which men were "ordained" in the apostolic times, deacon and elder, unless you add that of missionary evangelist. An illustration of the first is found in Acts 6, and the second, Acts 14:23. The case of the missionary evangelist is in Acts 13. To be sure Paul, in writing to Timothy, speaks of "bishops" and "deacons," (1 Timothy 3), which leads some to think that there were three such offices in the church of the New Testament—bishops or overseers, elders or presbyters, and deacons. The Roman Catholic Church, the Church of England, and the Protestant Episcopal Church hold to this three-fold order of the ministry, and will doubtless continue to do so till Jesus comes to translate the church to be with Him in the air; but although an Episcopalian, I am inclined to agree with the majority of the Protestant scholars that bishop and elder are one and the same order or office.

**May a hearer receive good from a minister not chosen of God, i. e., will the words of such an one have the same effect upon a sinner as those of one who is truly called and chosen?**

If I were to lay down a general principle in the matter I should certainly answer no. But there are exceptions to every rule, and God is sovereign, we must remember, in all His actings. He can make the wrath of man to praise Him, and He once used an ass to rebuke a prophet. So He may if He please, use a very unworthy instrument to bring about a very blessed deed, but such is not His usual course in the matter under present consideration. Certainly if the sinner was aware of the worldly character of the minister the latter would be unlikely to have any influence over him for good.

**Where in the Bible does it teach that a man must have some human ordination before he can minister at the Lord's Supper? Is it not the right and privilege of every brother in Christ to minister there, if so led by the Holy Spirit to do so?**

I know of no place in the Bible which forbids any Christian administering the Lord's Supper, ordination or no ordination; but we need be careful that liberty in this matter, as in some other matters, does not become license. God is not a God of confusion but of peace; therefore, let all things be done decently and in order. Some of the most serious heresies and wildest disorders in the church have claimed the leading of the Holy Spirit on the part of their advocates and representatives.

Let us remember that while God leads us as individuals, He also leads us as the corporate body of Christ. He makes known His mind to me as a member of that body through other of its members; and what He says to me needs to be qualified at times by what He says to others. It is generally safe in these matters of church order and discipline to stick close to what the church at large in all the centuries has regarded as the wise, safe and Scriptural course. "Come-outers" are not always deserving of as much praise as they imagine.

**Does 2 John 9-11 mean that a devout Christian should not entertain unbelieving friends and strangers, or does it mean that such are not to be received for the discussion of anti-Christian ideas?**

The latter is meant rather than the former, and yet the question is so serious that it can not be answered in a single sentence. This second epistle of John, being addressed to a

Christian woman, suggests that in this command of the apostle to her he has in mind the same thing as that of which Paul speaks in 2 Timothy 3:6, about false teachers creeping into houses and leading captive "silly women," i. e., as another puts it, "Calculating on their greater receptivity and mouldableness." The very fact that John refers to their not bringing "this doctrine" with them, shows that he has in mind those who are coming not as friends merely, or persons in need, but as false teachers. And not bringing "this doctrine" implies farther, that they are bringing a contrary doctrine.

Such are not to be received into the house of the true Christian, i. e., they are not to be received in their capacity as teachers. Of course, this would not preclude giving them to eat or a place to sleep if they were in need of either, for that would seem to contradict such plain teaching as Roman 12:13, 20 and other places.

Nor is the Christian to bid such an one welcome, which is scarcely different from the other command. "Joy, good speed, prosperity can not be said to the false teacher." He may be saluted after the conventional forms of politeness or ordinary friendship, but this is different from fraternal intercourse. The latter is as truly forbidden today, in such cases as it was in John's day, and is not to be attributed to intolerance but to true brotherly love in the truth.

"For he that biddeth him welcome partaketh of his evil deeds"; in other words, he is fostering a communion or fellowship with him which is itself sin, and harmful to the cause he is supposed to represent.

The correspondent will suffer me to suggest that this teaching seems to apply to many of the so-called "union" meetings often held in these days in the name of religion, where representatives of other faiths than the evangelical are assigned to places on the program as if such differences of doctrine were of no account. This may seem like charity to man, but it savors of treason to Christ.

### Written, or extempore sermons?

The suggestion has come that a word of instruction and advice be given to young ministers on the subject of written or extempore sermons. It is hardly within the scope of "Bible problems and difficulties," and yet an exception may be pardoned in the case of a subject so closely related thereto.

To begin with, let no young minister try to persuade himself that great preachers never preach from manuscript. Chalmers so preached, Baron Stowe so preached, Henry Ward Beecher so preached, Theodore L. Cuyler, William M. Taylor, Phillips Brooks so preached, not always, but frequently, and perhaps most of the time.

Neither let it be supposed that such preaching is unlikely to be accompanied by the power of the Holy Ghost.

Dr. Norman Macleod was once preaching in a district in Ayrshire, where the reading of a sermon is regarded as the greatest fault of which a minister can be guilty. When the congregation dispersed, an old woman overflowing with enthusiasm, addressed her neighbor, "Did ye ever hear onything sae gran'? Was na that a sermon?" But all her expressions of admiration being met by stolid silence, she shouted, "Speak, woman! Was na that a sermon?" "Ou aye," replied her friend, sulkily, "but he read it." "Read it!" said the other, with indignant emphasis, "I wadna hae cared if he had whustled it!"

I was about to say neither does God care if we "whustle" it. The question is, Are we surrendered to God? Are we filled with the Holy Ghost? The manner and method are, of course, not unimportant, but God is sovereign in His actings, and people differ in their tastes, and He is able to cause us to become all things to all men, that we may by all means save some (1 Corinthians 9:19-23).

As a matter of fact, every young minister should write, and perhaps read, at least one sermon a week for the first several years of his ministry. It will put a curb on verbosity, train him to close thinking, chasten his rhetoric, and contribute to variety in his pulpit utterances. His chirography, however, needs to be looked after. Many ministers write so poorly as to be unable to read their manuscript with ease, which accounts very largely for the prejudice against that style of preaching. Some of the clergymen named above had their material so well in hand when they entered the pulpit, that strangers in the congregation were not always aware that they were reading their sermons.

For a beginner to extemporize, the best plan is to attempt it on expository sermons. There you have a long text before you, and as Mr. Moody once said, "If you are persecuted in one verse, you can flee into another." The writer's general plan is to select his text and get his theme, after prayer to the Holy Spirit, early in the week, and commence thinking about it and praying over it right away. He carries the subject about with him wherever he goes, not as a detective shadowing him, but a friendly companion talking with him. He thinks of it, and goes over it, and works out its details while attending to other things. He consults books as may be necessary and as opportunity offers, looks up illustrations, fastens them in his mind, and practically puts the whole sermon together just as he will preach it, without writing a word. This seems to give him much of the accuracy of the written sermon, with all the extempore freedom he desires.

The disadvantage is that the sermon is soon lost to his memory so that he can not use it again; but this can be obviated by writing it out, in whole or in part, afterward, if one desires and has the time and patience to do it.

## CHAPTER VI.

### QUESTIONS ON CHRISTIAN DOCTRINE AND LIFE.

**How would you define the difference between soul and spirit? Since the fall, do we have the three-fold nature, the same as Adam did?**

It is difficult, if not impossible, to define the difference between soul and spirit. That there is a difference, however, seems evident from the following scriptures: Genesis 2:7; 1 Thessalonians 5:23 and Hebrews 4:12. From the first-named passage it would appear as if the soul were in some sense the product of the union between the dust of the ground and the breath or spirit of life. Some psychologists describe the three parts of man thus: The body is the seat of his sense-consciousness, the soul the seat of his self-consciousness, and the spirit the seat of his God-consciousness.

I see no reason to doubt that since the fall man retains the same three-fold nature, though on account of the entrance of sin his spiritual life, or God-consciousness, has become practically dead. His self-consciousness controls him in his natural state.

**Did Christ pay the penalty of the broken law, or did His death only suspend it and purchase a probation for mankind?**

We may thank God that Christ's death paid the penalty. See Acts 13:38, 39; Romans 8:1; Galatians 3:13 and many other places. If He had only purchased a probation for us, who could be saved? Adam was the only man ever on probation, and this in circumstances of innocence, yet he failed. What hope then would we have?

## Please explain the meaning of the "scapegoat" as mentioned in Leviticus 16.

In the Revised Version the word for scapegoat is the proper noun "Azazel," which some regard as the name of an evil spirit represented as dwelling in the wilderness, to which this goat, laden with Israel's sins, is sent. This evil spirit is conceived of as Satan, and the sending of the goat to him is an announcement that with the expiation of the sin of Israel through the sacrificial blood, his power over Israel is gone. Thus the acceptance of the blood of the one goat offered in the holy of holies symbolized the complete propitiation of God and his pardon of Israel's sin, while the sending of the other to Azazel symbolized the effect of this expiation in the complete removal of all the penal effects of sin through deliverance from the power of Satan as the executioner of God's wrath.

Others think the sending away of the goat to Satan laden with Israel's sins, represents Christ as our Sin-Bearer, deserted by His Father for a season, and delivered for His "bruising" into Satan's hand.

A simpler idea than either is that which employs the word not as a proper but an abstract noun meaning "removal" or "dismissal." In this case the goat bears away all the iniquities of Israel into the solitary land, representing their removal from the presence of God forever (Psalm 103:12; Micah 7:9). Thus the first goat, that which was slain, represents the means of reconciliation with God, and the second, the effect of that reconciliation. The two jointly constitute the sin-offering and set before us the atonement of Christ.

## What is it to believe on Christ unto salvation, and how may I know that my faith is genuine?

Saving faith is a cord of three threads, viz.: knowledge, assent, trust. You know there is a life-preserver under your berth at sea, you assent to the fact that if placed around your body it will keep you afloat in water, you trust it to do so when the vessel is sinking and you actually attach it to your body and plunge into the sea. A man knows that Jesus Christ is the Son of God, he assents to the fact that if he believes on Him he will be saved, but a day comes when under deep conviction of sin, and in the fear of hell he actually casts himself upon Him for help, renouncing every other allegiance. Some would say this last only is saving faith, and there is a sense in which such is true, and yet it presupposes the other two.

Our faith is genuine if based upon God's promises, but a cumulative proof of its genuineness is found in our growth in grace.

### May one who has no assurance lay claim to the new birth?

The new birth is not based on our assurance or consciousness of it, but on our faith in Christ. And yet if one were really believing God's promises to him it would seem that he must have some degree of assurance. Read in this connection 1 John 5:9-12.

And then there is another thought. A man who is born again is exhibiting "the fruit of the Spirit" (Galatians 5:22), and that ought to bring a consciousness that the change has taken place.

### How can people believe they have a thing until they know they have it?

In other words, the correspondent wishes to know how one can believe he is saved until he knows he is saved? Of course he can not believe it till he knows it; but he knows it the moment he believes, because to believe is to take God at His word. A person knows he owns a piece of ground because the deed of that ground to him is recorded in the court house, and he really knows it in no other way. Just so a man knows he is saved because it is recorded in the Word of God that whosoever accepts Jesus Christ as his Savior is saved, and he has accepted Jesus Christ. We know we are saved, not because we feel it, but because God has said it. Read 1 John 5:9-13.

### If Christ can save all, why are not all saved?

Not only is it true that Christ can save all, but as a matter of fact, He has already redeemed all by His blood. He is "the Lamb of God, which taketh away the sin of the world." (See also 1 John 2:2.) The only things standing in the way of the salvation of all men are, first, a knowledge of Jesus Christ as their Savior, and secondly, a willingness to accept Him as such. The first suggests the responsibility of saved men to make the Gospel known to the unsaved, and the second raises the question whether my inquirer has yielded his will to Christ on this last question. See the words of Jesus in John 5:40 and 7:17 (R. V.).

### How should you help a Unitarian to see salvation in Jesus Christ?

The same as I should help any other sinner. I should ask him if he were saved? And if he replied in the affirmative, I should ask on what he grounded his conviction? If he replied, "The finished work of Christ on the cross," he would not be a Unitarian. If he replied in any other way I should show him the truth in such passages as John 14:6, Acts 4:12 and Ephesians 2:8, 9. But probably he would say he did not need to be saved, in which case I should bring to his attention such passages as Romans 3:9-20. The Word of God and prayer are the only efficacious means of bringing any soul to Christ.

### If Adam had been punished with spiritual death, why was sentence in Genesis 3:17 pronounced against him?

This is something that man can not answer. The Judge of all the earth that does right ordained it so, but we may believe that hard as it seems love prompted it, and that in the end it will work out in the greater blessing to those who through faith in the promises humbly submit themselves to the decree. For one thing, it keeps us ever impressed with and alive to the reality of the curse upon sin, which without some such physical experience might be forgotten. It fosters the desire also, to be rid of sin, and leads us to inquire concerning the way out.

### How should you explain Romans 5:13?

Romans 5:13 reads, "For until the law sin was in the world, but sin is not imputed when there is no law." The first use of the word "law" here refers to the law given to Moses on Mount Sinai, at least 2,500 years after the fall of Adam. Now until this law was given sin was in the world. The law did not bring in sin. It was in before, all the time from Adam to Moses. All this time God treated men as sinners, and they were sinners. "But sin is not imputed where there is no law." Hence inasmuch as sin was imputed unto men, charged against men all that long time, there must have been some law revealed to them and resting upon them. Not the law of Sinai, indeed, but some other law from God. The law written on their consciences and the law He had revealed to them in other ways. The opening chapters of Genesis reveal many laws which God had given to men before Sinai, the violation of which was sin.

### Why is the Gospel of Christ good news? Or, more particularly, wherein is a man, truly penitent, more blessed under the new dispensation than under the old dispensation of the law?

Paul answers this question, in large part, when in Romans 3 he says, "By the law is the knowledge of sin." The law enables us to know what sin is, but it does not take away the sin it reveals. Only Christ does that through the Gospel. And this was as true in the old as it is in the new dispensation. Men were not saved by keeping the law in the days of Moses, for none of them kept it. They were saved through faith in Christ as expressed in their whole sacrificial system which pointed to and typified Him. This is not to say that they knew Him anticipatively, which doubtless was not true of but few of them; but they exercised faith in the offerings for sin they were directed to present, and this, in their ignorance was accepted as faith in him, since it was acting up to the measure of light they had. There were some, however, who were vouchsafed glimpses of the noonday radiance of revealed truth which we enjoy. Moses, for example, esteemed "the reproach of Christ greater riches than the treasures in Egypt," and God "preached before the gospel unto Abraham."

### On what grounds were the ancients saved?

In other words, the correspondent wishes to know whether the faith in a Christ who was to come had the same saving value as faith in a Christ who has come? The answer is in the affirmative. That is to say, all the Old Testament saints were saved on the basis of Christ's atonement. That atonement had not yet been rendered as an actual historical fact, but it had been accomplished nevertheless in the mind and purpose of God from the beginning. Christ was the lamb foreshadowed before the foundation of the world (1 Peter 1:20). To be sure, the faith of the fathers was not as intelligent as ours, they only saw these things afar off and were persuaded of them, but man is saved not on the ground of a faith tested by its intellectual but its moral quality. A good passage bearing on the subject which it would be well for the correspondent to read is Romans 4, especially verses 16-25.

### Will you give me the Scriptural proof that all infants dying in infancy are saved?

There is no "Scriptural proof." We hope they are saved through the mercy of God on the ground of the atonement of Christ; and this inasmuch as, although they were born in sin, they were not actual transgressors of God's law.

### Do not Matthew 18:10 and Luke 18:16 prove that all infants dying in infancy are saved?

Those utterances of Jesus give us strong reason to hope that such is the case, but it is not generally thought that they amount to absolute proof of that fact.

The correspondent seems a little confused in employing the fact that God is no respecter of persons, to defend the opinion that all will be saved; but if he means simply that if one infant is saved all infants will be saved, then I am happy to be able to agree with him.

### Where do children who die before the age of accountability go at death?

Every Christian hopes and believes that they go to heaven on the ground of Christ's general atonement for sin. But no one is able to speak positively on that point because the Scriptures do not speak positively upon it. There is much in the Scriptures from which we may draw such an inference, but farther than this we can not go.

### Please explain 1 John 2:12 in relation to infant salvation.

The phrase "little children," in that case does not refer to infants or babes, but as the Greek word indicates, it means "dear children." They were the apostle's own children in the faith whom he thus addresses in terms of endearment, although they may have reached years of maturity. See Jesus' address to his disciples (John 21:5).

### Will heathen, having received no knowledge of the Word, and dying without believing on Christ whom they know not, be lost forever?

All men are lost because of sin, heathen included. Christ is the only remedy for sin, and it is our urgent duty to make Him known to the uttermost parts of the earth; but men are not condemned for not having known Him where they have never had the opportunity to do so. It is like disease in the human body, for which there is a certain cure, but of which the afflicted one in a certain case has no knowledge. He dies because of the disease.

This solemn subject is set before us very clearly in the first chapter of Romans, and ought to be understood by every Christian. Read that chapter from verse 16 to the end, but especially verses 18 to 25, and you will see that the heathen in his darkness is "without excuse." Had he lived up to the light he had, more would have been given him, but this he has failed to do with the result that deeper darkness has settled upon him. Cornelius, mentioned in Acts 10, is an instance of a heathen who lived up to the light and received more, even a knowledge of Christ; and wherever this type of man is found in any nation or age, there like blessing comes to him.

Some are inclined to charge God with unfairness to the heathen world in not making Christ known to them as well as us, but we need to remember that God was under no obligation to make Him known even to us. And now that He has done so, it is that we may make Him known to the whole world. How have we fulfilled our obligation, or what are we doing in that direction? Until we, as a church, have exhausted our last resource to carry the Gospel to the heathen, it ill becomes us to charge unkindness upon God.

### Why was Esau rejected and Jacob chosen, and was Esau saved?

Esau was rejected and Jacob chosen not because of any moral difference in the two men, but on the ground of God's sovereign pleasure. But the choice, it should be remembered, was not as to eternal life, that is, heaven or hell, but only with reference to the promised earthly seed. Esau was not "hated" in the sense of divine vindictive anger against him, but only in that he was set aside for this particular purpose. He led what was a happy life for him, was much prospered in earthly things, and we may hope was "saved" eternally as truly as his brother. That is, I do not think the record teaches necessarily that he was lost.

**What is regeneration, in its broadest sense? And does a regenerated soul have a desire for worldly amusement?**

Regeneration, in its broadest sense and only sense is life —life in Christ Jesus, through a new birth in a spiritual sense, by the operation of the Holy Spirit, through the exercise of our faith in Christ as our Savior. The natural man is dead in trespasses and sins, dead to God, to holiness, to eternal happiness, to hope of heaven. "Except a man be born again, he cannot see the kingdom of God" (John 3:3) But when he becomes thus born again, "old things are passed away, and all things are become new" (2 Corinthians 5:17). His old selfish, carnal views of things, of himself, of others, of the world—even of Christ, spontaneously melt away like snow before the summer sun. He will not desire, much less delight, in worldly amusements. At the same time we must remember that there are "babes" in Christ, and that there is such a thing as "growth in grace."

Some do not lose all desire for worldly amusements as speedily or thoroughly as others. And there is a fair difference of opinion among really true Christians as to what constitutes a "worldly amusement." In the writer's opinion, however, it is well to give the interests of one's soul, and the cause of Jesus Christ the benefit of any doubt which one may have about it (Romans 14:23).

**Which is experienced first, faith or repentance?**

While there is a distinction in thought between these two, there is scarcely any distinction in time. Repentance means a "change of mind," and the moment one takes Jesus by faith to be his personal Savior, that moment he has experienced and manifested that change of mind. I am now speaking, of course, of the initial act of salvation. But

It is true that even to the saved soul there is a sense in which repentance is a continuous experience, and the same may be said of faith. There is a definite moment when we repent and believe on the Lord Jesus Christ and are saved; and yet as we grow in the Christian life we are ever coming to see more and more clearly what sin is, and what a savior Jesus is, and in that measure is our repentance ever deepening and our faith ever increasing.

### May a man be justified and sanctified at the same time?

There is a sense in which this may be answered in the affirmative, depending upon the meaning attached to the word "sanctified." The word has two meanings, one expressing a condition into which the believer is brought before God on the instant in which he so believes; the other expressing his experience and manifestation of that condition in his daily life, which is a matter of time. Perhaps a good illustration of the first is found in 1 Corinthians 6:11, and of the second in 1 Thessalonians 5:23.

### When and where was Paul sanctified?

Speaking of sanctification as a state or condition of a man legally or judicially before God, Paul was sanctified at the same moment he was justified, and perhaps that was when he yielded himself to Christ on the way to Damascus (Acts 9). Then he was set apart for God's use and service forever, and then, in that sense, he was sanctified. But speaking of sanctification as an experience of holiness in a man's heart and a manifestation of it in his daily life, then Paul was in the constant process and progress of it to the end of his life. Such utterances of his as Philippians 3:12-14 and 1 Timothy 1:15 would seem to indicate this.

### Is eradiction the Scriptural teaching on holiness?

I believe not. It contradicts the Scriptures rather, for example, 1 John 1:8-10. It also contradicts experience, for example, that of Paul (1 Timothy 1:15). Indeed, the experience of Paul is that of all enlightened Christians, I believe. Christian growth largely consists in putting away sin as it is increasingly revealed to us. The holier a believer becomes the more clearly he perceives the real nature of sin, not sin in the abstract, or sin in somebody else, but sin in his own life. If I am a growing Christian, what is sin to me now was not such perhaps a year ago, and so it will continue to be to the end.

There are those who profess eradication to have taken place in their lives, but as a rule their neighbors do not agree with them, I think. Their mistake lies in a very limited appreciation of what sin is. They base their claim, from a Scriptural point of view, chiefly on such passages as 1 John 3:6, 9, but these are to be interpreted in the light of the two natures in the believer. The new nature in Christ Jesus does not sin, but the old nature is ever warring against it, and only in the measure in which the believer is yielding himself to the indwelling Spirit of God will he be able to overcome in the continual conflict (Galatians 5:17, R. V.). Thus, however, he will be able to overcome so that he may live every day a victor over all known sin; but this is something different from the eradication of all sin.

**What is the meaning of 2 Peter 1:10, about making our "calling and election sure"?**

It means making our calling and election sure, not as far as God is concerned, but with reference to our own experience of it. If God has called and chosen us to be saved in Christ, He is sure of it. But we also may be sure by bringing forth in our Christian lives the graces and fruits named in the preceding verses of that chapter. We can do this by yielding ourselves to the work of the Holy Spirit in us from day to day.

**Is that saying true, "Once in grace, always in grace," or, if a man is truly converted, accepts**

Christ, and is regenerated, can he commit sin that will cause him to lose his soul?

I should not like to say what he "could" do, but I have a good deal of confidence in saying what I think he "would" do, viz.: remain steadfast unto the end and enter into the fulness of salvation in glory. I believe this, not because I have any confidence in the man himself even after he is saved, but because I have every confidence in God's promise, and purpose, and power to glorify His Son in perfecting the good work He has begun (Philippians 1:6). The course for a saved man to pursue, who may through infirmity, or ignorance or stress of temptation fall into sin, is laid down for him in 1 John 1:9. The reference to 1 John 5:18, which the inquirer makes, affords an opportunity to say that the inspired writer is there speaking of the new nature in the regenerated man. The latter has two natures, the old Adam nature, called the "flesh," in which dwells no good thing (Romans 7:18), and the new Christ nature which is created in true holiness and righteousness (Ephesians 4:24), and which does not commit sin. These two are contrary the one to the other (Galatians 5:17), and sin on the part of the Christian consists in allowing the old nature to obtain the upper hand of the new, which never need be the case if he will yield himself to the influences of the Holy Spirit who dwells within him to give him the victory (Romans 7:24, 25, and chapter 8).

A correspondent says, that at one time in his life he deliberately rejected Christ, and firmly believes his soul is now lost. His horror and anguish are great. His pastor and other Christian friends tell him he is mistaken. He has spent hours in prayer about it, without avail, and he asks whether there is hope for him?

I think there is hope for him. His letter does not indicate that he has rejected Christ as he thinks he has done; and his pastor and other Christian advisers who know him better than I, are doubtless wise in their opinion about him. Satan would seem to be disturbing his mind. The God I know and worship in Jesus Christ, will not turn a deaf ear to one who pleads for hours for salvation through the blood of his Son. Let him repent, and accept Jesus Christ as his Savior now, confessing Him as such before men. The feeling or assurance may not come to him that he is saved, but he is not saved by feeling or assurance. He is saved by Christ. "Though he slay me, yet will I trust in him." "Him that cometh to me I will in no wise cast out."

**Please explain the two-fold use of the word "perfect" in Philippians 3:12 and 15."**

The writer will be aided to understand the different uses of the word "perfect" here, if he keeps in mind that the inspired apostle is using throughout the figure of a race course, such as those covered by the foot runners in the Olympian games. In verse 15, "as many as are perfect," means as many as are experienced, full-grown, no longer babes in the Christian life (1 Corinthians 2:6), and hence fully equipped for running the race. They know and are able to comply with the laws of the course (2 Timothy 2:5). But in verse 12, not as though I "were already perfect," means not as though I were yet the actual winner of the race. I am not yet crowned with victory. Absolute perfection is meant in the last case (verse 12), relative perfection in the first (verse 15).

**What is your teaching on sanctification, the Spirit-filled life, and receiving the Holy Ghost as a second distinctive work of grace? And does this work take out of us the old Adam nature, the root of bitterness, and leave us pure and holy in God's sight?**

Sanctification has two meanings. The moment we believe on Jesus Christ we are sanctified in the sense that we are then set apart for God forever. But at the same moment the Holy Spirit takes up His dwelling in us and begins a process of sanctification in the experimental sense, as the result of which we grow in grace and in the knowledge of God.

The indwelling of the Holy Spirit is equivalent to our baptism into the body of Christ, and is a single transaction taking place once and forever. But it is one thing thus to have the Holy Spirit dwelling in us, and another to be filled with the Holy Spirit. There is but one indwelling, while there may be many fillings of the Spirit.

In the sense of the indwelling, therefore, there is no second distinctive work of grace to be expected; but in the sense of the filling of the Spirit there may be many such experiences.

This does not take out of us the old Adam nature, but gives us power through the new nature to overcome the old, and live a life of victory over known sin. It does not make us pure and holy in God's sight in the sense that we have no experience of sin; but when we believe on Christ we become pure and holy in God's sight in the sense that thereafter there is no sin on us. He takes away its guilt, but as long as we remain in this body there will be a consciousness of sin in us, and a deepening feeling of unworthiness because of it.

### What does the New Testament teach about the second work of grace and the baptism of the Holy Ghost?

I believe the teaching of the New Testament to be that when one receives the Lord Jesus Christ as his Savior, being regenerated by the Holy Spirit, he is then baptized by the same Spirit into the body of which Christ is the head. Compare Acts 1:5; 2:1-4; 1 Corinthians 12:13; Ephesians 4:4-6.

I believe that the second work of grace, of which some people speak, is a later crisis in the history of the believer when he comes to realize the need of a holier life, and a deeper experience in Christ. He then surrenders himself as a Christian to Christ more fully than he had yet done, and comes into the Spirit, to which he had been a stranger theretofore. His spiritual life now takes on a new aspect, and he becomes more truly separated from sin and quickened in the service of his Lord.

It is the privilege of every believer to have this experience at the moment of his acceptance of Christ as a Savior, and some do enter into its enjoyment then. Many do not, however, and when it comes to them, if it does, they regard it as a second work of grace and baptism of the Holy Spirit.

As a matter of fact, however, there is but one baptism of the Holy Spirit, and the richer experiences referred to are those which grow out of it, when the soul is truly surrendered to God, who by His Spirit thus dwells within.

### What is the meaning of "the sin not unto death" (1 John 5:17)?

In my judgment, it is any other sin than the deliberate and final rejection of Jesus Christ. Compare Matthew 12:31, 32, where the blasphemy against the Holy Ghost, or the unpardonable sin, is the rejection of the testimony of the Holy Ghost to Christ, and hence the final rejection of Christ.

There is another view of this passage, however, which takes the ground that the reference is not to spiritual but physical death. The one referred to in the text is a Christian brother who has been chastised by sickness on account of sin. But the sinning not having been unto death (physical death), he is raised up. "However, a believer may go on wilfully sinning and remain there dishonoring Christ. He is to be taken out of the world by death. No request could be made for such an one." (See Gaebelein's *Commentary on Matthew* at 12:31, 32.)

### What is the unpardonable sin?

There are at least three passages in the New Testament which may be in mind when asking this question. The first in Matthew 12:31, 32, and the parallel places in the other Gospels, where the "unpardonable sin" seems to consist in attributing to Satan the work of the Holy Spirit. The second is Hebrews 6:4-6, where it consists in total apostacy from Christianity and a return to Judaism, as the teaching of the epistle as a whole seems to indicate. The third is 1 John 5:16, where the application would seem to be limited by the meaning of the other two passages just referred to.

I would explain this last sentence thus: Since the Holy Spirit through John does not define specifically what He means by the "sin unto death," it seems reasonable to suppose that He would have us seek its definition in other places in the Scriptures where He does so define it, and those places are the ones mentioned.

Some, however, would interpret 1 John 5:16 in a different way. They would say that some men are incorrigible sinners, that they have reached, even in this life, a permanent condition of sin which is apparent beyond question to Christians of true spiritual enlightenment, and that the latter are here relieved from the obligation to pray for forgiveness in such cases. There will be differences of opinion as to this interpretation, but in any event it suggests this further definition of the "unpardonable sin," that, no matter what else it consists in, it certainly does in this, viz.: The failure in this life to receive Jesus Christ by faith as a personal Savior. The man who dies unsaved notwithstanding Christ has been offered to him as a Savior, commits the unpardonable sin. There is no forgiveness or salvation for him in the world to come. This is the most practical and general application of this whole subject.

It answers also a second question as to "what is meant by a person having sinned away his day of grace?" The present Gospel dispensation is "the day of grace" (2 Corinthians 6:2), and the expression, for that reason, applies as well to the earthly lifetime of every man who does not deliberately and of free choice reject the offer of salvation through Christ.

### How is the expression in Exodus 33:19 and Romans 9:15 to be understood?

I should say that the expression of Exodus 33:19, and Romans 9:15, "I will have mercy on whom I will have mercy," is to be taken literally. All men are sinners by nature, and of their own free will, and grace is unmerited favor. God is at liberty to save some if He will, and whom He will, but there is no obligation upon Him to save one, much less all. At the same time His salvation is freely and sincerely offered to all who will accept it by faith. It is admitted that there is profound mystery here before which we can only bow our heads and wait, but that is the attitude of faith, and the attitude that becomes the finite in the presence of the Infinite.

### How may 1 John 1:8 and 1 John 2:1 be harmonized with 1 John 3:8, 9, and 1 John 5:18?

These passages may be harmonized, I believe, on the ground of the two natures in the Christian believer. That which is born of God is the new nature in Christ Jesus, and does not of itself commit sin. But the old nature still remains, the flesh, as it is called, which lusteth or warreth against the Spirit, i. e., the Holy Spirit (Galatians 5:17). As a Christian yields or surrenders himself to the Holy Spirit he receives power to overcome the old nature and to live a life of victory over known sin. But the old nature is still there whose presence justifies the words of John in the earlier chapter of his epistle.

### What do you understand by the "lawful use of the law"?

The inquirer is doubtless referring to 1 Timothy 1:8, where the apostle says: "The law is good, if a man use it lawfully." Paul is speaking of certain Judaizing teachers in the early church who corrupted the moral law of God by "fables which they pretended to found upon it, subversive of morals as well as truth." "Their error," to quote the *Bible Commentary*, "was not in maintaining the obligation of the law, but in abusing it by fabulous and immoral interpretations and additions to it." "The law is good," the apostle explains, i. e., it is in full agreement with God's holiness and goodness, "if a man use it lawfully," if he gives it its lawful place in the Gospel economy; which place, he proceeds to indicate, is that of awakening the sense of sin in the ungodly (see verses 9 and 10). These false teachers doubtless, used the law as a means by which a justified man might attain higher perfection in Christ than by the Gospel of faith alone. But this was wrong, since "the law brings with it no inward power to fulfill it."

And yet, is there no sense whatsoever, in which a justified man morally needs the law? Certainly there is. He needs it not as a ground or procuring cause either of salvation or sanctification, but just as he needed it as a means by which he came to see his need of salvation as a sinner, so he needs it as a means by which he may come to see his need of sanctification as a saint. I mean his experimental sanctification.

By "the law" now I do not intend simply the Ten Commandments, but all that God has revealed to us of his will in His Word. How can a man be holy who knows not what holiness is? And who can tell him what it is, save God? And where does God tell him if not in His law?

This is the trouble with many who profess a holiness which their neighbors perceive they do not possess. The holiness they profess is their own idea of holiness, not God's idea. If they were better acquainted with the law of God and used it "lawfully," they would put their mouths in the dust with a sense of their uncleanness.

### What is the inheritance which God has in the saints (Ephesians 1:18)?

I suppose that such other verses in that same epistle as 1:12; 2:7, 22; 3:10; 4:13; 5:27, etc., explain what it is as well as it can be explained to our present understanding, and until the time when we who only know in part shall know "even as we are known." The great thought is that God has an inheritance in us. This does not exclude the thought of our inheritance in Him, but the other is the stronger and more precious of the two. If we had an inheritance in God it is conceivable that we might fail of its possession, but if God has an inheritance in us then we are persuaded that He is able to keep that which is His own.

Moreover, God's inheritance in us implies the execution in us and towards us of great purposes of grace and glory to make us what He would have us become as worthy of Him. These are the hints which are given us in the above quoted passages as intimating the nature of His inheritance.

**Please explain Ephesians 4:5, about union with Christ.**

"One Lord, one faith, one baptism," refers to the unity of believers in Christ. They have "one Lord," or one Head over them, the Lord Jesus Christ. They have "one faith," or one act of believing by which they apprehended or laid hold of Him for salvation. And they have "one baptism," or sacrament by which they are incorporated, or express their incorporation in the body of Christ. By this "one baptism" some would understand that of water, but I prefer to regard it as the baptism of the Holy Spirit which took place on the Day of Pentecost, and in which the whole church is, in a sense, included. It is to this that Paul refers in 1 Corinthians 12:13.

**Please explain Romans 6:4, as to the mode of baptism Paul has in mind.**

Paul is probably not referring to the "mode" but to the thing itself. In reading the verse we should not put a comma after baptism, but read right on, "baptism into death." Our baptism into Christ' death is our spiritual identification with Him in His death (see verse 8). This identification with Him takes place the instant we believe on Him as our Savior. The water or ritual baptism which follows the exercise of our faith is an outward sign or symbol of that faith, and those who practice baptism by immersion believe that immersion best symbolizes our identification with Christ in His death and resurrection. Of course, the other side does not accept this view, and does not regard the mode of baptism as of so much importance.

Answers to two or three correspondents about baptism and salvation are given in the following paragraphs.

As to the teaching about baptism in Romans 6:3, 4, my conviction is that the inspired apostle is not referring to water baptism at all, but to that baptism by the Holy Spirit, by which we enter into Christ, i. e., become members of His body (see 1 Corinthians 12:13). And in Romans 6:3 particularly, of which one of the correspondents asks, "Paul does indeed teach that we must be baptized into Jesus Christ in order to be saved, but he does not say we must be baptized into water." The baptism into Jesus Christ is that just referred to above, by the Spirit.

As to 1 Peter 3:21, I do not understand it to teach that water baptism is essential to salvation, because if it did teach that it would be in opposition to other scriptures which teach differently. And yet so far as it refers to water baptism at all, it indicates the obligation resting upon those who are saved through faith in Christ to submit to the outward rite of baptism as a sign or symbol of that fact and of their new relationship to Him.

As to the question whether water baptism signifies or symbolizes the outpouring of the Spirit or our identification with Christ in His death and resurrection, I am inclined to the latter view, and yet we can not close our eyes to the fact that we do really become thus identified with Christ only through the outpouring of the Holy Spirit upon us.

**Were the nine gifts of the Spirit in 1 Corinthians 12:8-11 permanent gifts to the church?**

They seem to have been so with, perhaps, the exception of the last two, and yet greater familiarity with the history of missions might enable me to qualify even this remark. As for the other seven gifts we see them all in operation today. Knowledge of the Word of God is a distinct gift to some, and so is wisdom in the use of that Word and in the administration of the affairs of the church. Faith like George Müller's is such a gift. I think the annals of modern missions show something now and again corresponding to the "workings of miracles," or signs and powers in answer to prayer. Prophesying corresponds to preaching and testimony which is certainly a current and distinct gift.

**What are the strongest arguments in the favor of divine healing, and how may these be explained and met? Do you believe in miracle-working in this age?**

The strongest arguments are those from experience and Scripture. Among the latter especially James 5:14. While I am not a witness to the truth in my own experience, I nevertheless know others who are, and I have had satisfactory evidence presented to me that their witness is true. This is not to say that all which goes by the name of divine healing is entitled to that designation, neither is it to deny that there is much foolishness and fanaticism connected therewith; but that God heals now, when it pleases Him so to do, as He did in the days of Christ and His apostles, without the intervention of natural means or human agencies, is a fact that can not successfully be gainsaid. Let this fact be balanced by that other, that it is God who heals in any event, whether with means or without them, and much of the danger of fanaticism in that respect is past.

Perhaps I have said enough to satisfy the inquirer as to what I believe about miracle-working in the present age. God works miraculously wherever He pleases to do so, but it is often a lack of faith on our part which demands that He shall work miraculously for us. We should be careful, too, to distinguish between His work and the "lying wonders" of Satan and his emissaries. "By their fruits shall ye know them." "To the law and to the testimony; if they speak not according to this word, it is because there is no light in them."

**Why is not the preaching of the Gospel accompanied by signs and miracles, as is promised in Mark 16:17, 18? Is it not an undeniable fact that such demonstrations would bring about the conversion of many who are careless and filled with doubt? And would not Christians, too, be greatly strengthened in their faith?**

Here are three questions in one. As to the first, I reply that expositors are generally agreed that the promise in Mark refers primarily, if not specifically, to the apostolic age, when such miracles were necessary to arrest attention and affirm the divinity of the Gospel message. As time elapsed, however, such credentials were superseded by those of another kind, such as the fulfillment of prophecy, the growth and development of the church itself, the effects of the Gospel in the lives of individuals and in the history of nations, to say nothing of its self-evidencing character, as compared with the religions of paganism.

It may be added, however, that, even in our own day, such miracles as the passage refers to are not uncommon in the history of foreign missions, where the evidence they afford may be said to be necessary as in the first century.

The correspondent is wrong, however, in his statement that such demonstrations would result in the conversion of the careless and doubting. Miracles in themselves have no converting power, as may be seen in the history of the ministry of Christ Himself. Men saw the wonderful works He did and continued careless and unbelieving. (Compare Matthew 11:20 and Luke 16:31.)

As to the last question, Christians are not strengthened by miracles so much as by feeding upon the Word of God, ministered to them by the Spirit of God. Jesus rebuked some of His followers who were always looking for miracles. (Compare Acts 20:32 and Ephesians 3:16.)

**To what Person of the Godhead should Christians address their prayers?**

As there is only one God, it seems as though there need be no distinction on this point. As a matter of fact, God the Father is usually directly addressed in prayer, and yet Stephen prayed directly to Jesus (Acts 7). I recall no Bible illustrations of direct address to the Holy Spirit, but the liturgies and hymnody of the church are rich in them. By the term "Our Father," as used in the Lord's Prayer, I understand God to be meant as including the conception of the Trinity. Ephesians 2:18 should be read in connection with this subject however, in which we are taught that it is really to God the Father we pray through Jesus Christ, having access by the Holy Spirit.

**What is the proper interpretation of Romans 8:34, which speaks of the intercession of Jesus? For whom does He intercede, all mankind, or only His own believing people?**

The teaching of the Scriptures is that it is for the latter only. Hebrews 9:24 (R. V.) reads: "Christ entered not into a holy place made with hands, like in pattern to the true; but into heaven itself, now to appear before the face of God for us." As our High Priest in heaven He is:

1. The forerunner of His people. Hebrews 6:20.
2. The intercessor for His people. Hebrews 7:25.
3. The benefactor of His people. Ephesians 4:8.
4. The host of His people. John 14:2.

It is all for His own people it will be seen.

**Is not the application of Mark 16:14-16 limited to the eleven disciples?**

It looks so on the face of it, because Christ is there addressing them particularly, but the language of the commission itself would seem to imply that all His disciples, the whole church, were meant down to the end of the age. And then, too, there are other scriptures which corroborate this view, like Romans 10:13, 14.

## The Christian's obligation.

A correspondent says there are three things that trouble a good many Christian people to keep, one is,

### THE TEN COMMANDMENTS.

I confess I can not see where the trouble comes in here except in the case of the fourth commandment, which, unlike any of the others, is partly moral and partly ceremonial. On its moral side it belongs to all to keep it, on its ceremonial side it belonged distinctively to the Jews to keep it. On its moral side it calls for the setting apart of one day in seven for rest, on its ceremonial side a particular day is designated. Should it "trouble a good many Christian people" to give their bodies rest one day a week?

The second thing that troubles them to keep is part of

### THE SERMON ON THE MOUNT.

Which part is not specified, but probably those parts whose keeping presupposes not only regenerated men but a regenerated environment. The Sermon on the Mount, like the contents of the Old Testament, is primarily Jewish in its interpretation. It is a discourse on the kingdom which Christ came to set up on the earth. It describes the citizens of that kingdom, the laws to govern it, the way of entering into it, and so on. That kingdom has not yet been set up because the King was rejected by his people, but its time is coming. When it comes the Sermon on the Mount will be its constitution and its bill of rights. In the meantime, the New Testament epistles, especially those of Paul, contain the instructions for the government of the church. This is not to say that nothing in the Sermon on the Mount belongs to us Christians as an obligation. There are certain principles laid down there which apply to the saints of God in all ages and dispensations, but the application of divine principles differs with different ages. To perceive this, and square one's conduct in accordance with it, is to fulfill the inspired injunctions about "rightly dividing the word of truth," and giving to each their "portion of meat in due season."

The third thing found troubling to some is

THE ACTIVE MEMBER'S PLEDGE OF THE CHRISTIAN ENDEAVOR SOCIETY.

Again, I can not understand the trouble in the case of true Christians, except that they may have conscientious scruples against taking any kind of pledge which may seem to bind them to men or to a human organization. But the nature of the obligations in that pledge is what every disciple of Christ recognizes as necessary for his own spiritual life, to say nothing of any other motive.

### Under what circumstances is it right to be angry?

The writer quotes Ephesians 4:26, "Be ye angry, and sin not." Jesus was angry (Mark 3:5), but sinned not. As another puts it, "Our natural feelings are not wrong when directed to their legitimate object, and when not exceeding due bounds. For example, indignation at dishonor done to God and wrong to man is justifiable anger." It is passion that is sinful, because, as the word indicates, the man is "passive," i. e., the slave to his anger instead of ruling it. Hence, in Ephesians 4:26, the apostle goes on to say, "Let not the sun go down upon your wrath." Wrath is passion, it is irritation and exasperation mingling with anger, and we should put it away at once. Anger is not absolutely forbidden, but passion and wrath are. And yet "anger is like poison used in medicine, and needs to be handled with extreme care."

## CHAPTER VII.

### QUESTIONS ON APPLIED CHRISTIANITY.

**Is it right under any circumstances to ride on the train or street car on Sunday?**

That is a question every Christian prefers to answer for himself. The writer is not in the habit of using trains or cars for pleasure on Sunday, but he thinks he is at liberty to use them in the Lord's work on that day. Others feel that they may make additional exceptions. Read in this connection, Romans 14:1-8.

A friend is seeking light upon his duty as to certain aspects of the Sunday question. Cigars, candy, etc., are sold in his town on that day in violation of law. Moreover, some of the offenders are office-bearers in the church. The Sabbath Association has detectives spying out the law-breakers, and these secure evidence by making purchases of the culprits in disguise, which the correspondent considers "doing evil that good may come." The question is, What is his duty in the premises?

It is quite difficult to answer this question with any degree of satisfaction without knowing just how his individual responsibility comes most closely into contact with the situation. One thing ought to be clear, however, and that is that Christians and office-bearers in the church ought not to be violators of the law. One may have liberty of opinion as to the right or wrong of selling such articles on Sunday, but hardly on the question of obeying the mandates of the state. If the state says: "This is contrary to law," it is the plain duty of the citizen to yield obedience, and church-members who fail to do so are amenable both

## Applied Christianity

to the civil and ecclesiastical courts. Perhaps a little church discipline, meekly, but firmly administered in this case would be salutary.

As to the ethics in the method of obtaining the evidence, the world will probably be divided upon it for some time to come; nor is this a matter which seems to qualify in any way the guilt of the parties concerned. There may be a doubt as to whether the Sabbath Association is doing right, but there can be none that the Christian tradesman are doing wrong.

A correspondent asks a number of questions on the Sabbath, which may be answered without repeating them in detail:

1. The Ten Commandments are still binding upon Christians, not, however, as a ground or means of salvation, but a standard of righteousness they should seek by God's grace to attain.

2. Christ did not keep Sunday, the first day of the week, in any special way. He was a Jew, made under the law, and kept the Jewish Sabbath or seventh day of the week as a day of rest.

3. Sunday is nowhere spoken of in the New Testament as a holy day in so many words, but that it was kept as such by the apostolic church from the very first, is evident from such records as John 20:19, 26; Acts 20:7; 1 Corinthians 16:2, and Revelation 1:10.

4. It is not true that the Roman Catholic Church changed the day of rest from the seventh to the first day of the week, because the Roman Catholic Church, i. e., the papacy, did not begin to raise its head much before the sixth century, while the change to some degree had been observed by Christians, as we see, even in the days of the apostles. The reason for this change, in which the church seems to have had the guidance and blessing of the Spirit of God, was to commemorate the resurrection of Jesus Christ, who by that event became the Head of the body, the church

(Colossians 1:18). Thus the keeping of the first day of the week by Christians, instead of the seventh, becomes in itself one of the most convincing evidences, as it is a continual historic evidence, of the divine origin of Christianity as based upon the finished work of Christ. Furthermore, the claim that the papacy changed the day is not substantiated by the witness of the martyrs and reformers. They had many charges to lay at the door of the wicked hierarchy, for some of which they paid the penalty of their lives, but the changing of the day of rest was not one of them. Finally, all the holy men of old have kept the first day of the week as the day of rest. To mention some only of our own time, Leighton, Rutherford, McCheyne, Chalmers, the Bonars, the Haldanes, the Monods, Blumhardt, Krummacher, Mueller, Spurgeon, the Wesleys, Whitfield, Edwards, Brainard, Carey, Martyn, Judson, Livingstone, Taylor, and time would fail me to mention the rest. These men were filled with the Spirit of God, and did not wear the mark of the beast.

A correspondent is much troubled by some Seventh-Day Adventists recently preaching in his town, who claim, he says, that we ought to keep the seventh day instead of the first, and that those who do not so keep it have the "mark of the beast" upon them as spoken of in Revelation 13. He wishes to have that "mark" explained, and also the question about observing the seventh day.

The "Beast" spoken of in Daniel and the Revelation symbolizes that wicked despot known otherwise as the Antichrist, who is to arise at the end of the present age, and who shall be destroyed by the brightness of Christ's coming (2 Thessalonians 2). Until the "Beast" himself appears it is unlikely that his "mark" shall be known. Just what it will be we can not now say. But the brother may be assured that the keeping of the first day of the week as one of rest and worship in commemoration of Christ's resurrection from the dead, cannot be that mark. The keeping of that day exalts Christ, while it is the business and the purpose of the Antichrist to dethrone and dishonor Him. The inconsistency of such a charge, therefore, is glaring.

**Please summarize the doctrine of Seventh-Day Adventism, especially concerning Christ, the resurrection, and the judgment.**

The Seventh-Day Adventists believe in the Bible, in conversion, in purity of life, and in other good things common to all churches, but they reject the doctrine of the Trinity, which involves the Diety of Christ, though this is not stated. They believe that the end of the world is to come in this generation, and that they are called of God to give the last warning to the race. They believe that the dead are unconscious, and that the wicked, including the Devil, will be annihilated. They believe also that when Christ comes only 144,000 out of all then living will be saved, and that this number will be limited to themselves.

**What books would you recommend to help me to reply to the advocates of Seventh-Day Adventism?**

We would recommend you to read *Seventh-Day Adventism Renounced*, by Elder Canright, published by Revell, or a small pamphlet entitled, *Ought Christians to Keep the Sabbath?* by R. A. Torrey.

**Would Psalm 15:5 and other passages on usury indicate that the taking of interest, as now commonly practiced in the business world, is wrong?**

The word "usury" is commonly employed in the Bible in the sense of interest merely. We speak of "usurious interest," but the Bible never does, although the idea which those words suggest is that which the Bible has generally in mind when it uses the word usury. That usury in the sense of simple interest, however, is not in itself wrong, would seem to be the inference from such passages as Deuteronomy

23:20, where its imposition is permitted in the case of a stranger or foreigner to Israel. What the Bible is inculcating against usury, or interest, is its employment among the Hebrews themselves as fellow members of the theocracy, and especially in their dealings with the poor. Interest in itself, however, would seem to be a legitimate form of business, and only becomes illegitimate when it is excessive, or employed in a spirit contrary to that of the second table of the law—"Thou shalt love thy neighbor as thyself." Whether the business world of today violates this commandment or not in its demands for the loan of money, my correspondent is probably as well able to judge as I. When it does so it is guilty of usury in the bad sense, and it can not escape a day of settlement for its sins.

To add a further word, loan associations, it has been developed, could not do business on a smaller margin than 2 per cent per month. This might be regarded in some quarters as "usury," and yet to cut off the business of such associations would be to work injury instead of good to the people intended to be benefited. All of which teaches us the great wisdom required in the application of the principles of Christianity to the specific case, and how careful we should be about raising a cry of wrong-doing before we know the facts.

**Is the carrying of life insurance by a Christian in any way contrary to the teaching of the Bible, and would you apply the same principles to any other kind of insurance?**

The best answer I can give to this question is to say that I carry insurance both on my life and on my property, which I certainly should not do did I consider either contrary to the teaching of the Bible. It seems to me that 1 Timothy 5:8 may have a bearing upon the question.

The matter is a very serious one to many sensitive and conscientious Christians, and warrants a further word of brotherly counsel. There are those who feel that the life of faith means a disregard of the ordinary suggestions of natural reason and intelligence, and that to make provision for the earthly future of one's family is to doubt God and to retain the reins of government in one's own hands. But this is not so, necessarily. There may be isolated instances in every age and nation where God calls upon His witnesses to step forth into an extraordinary kind of experience like the patriarchs of the Old Testament or the apostles of the New, but I feel satisfied that they are isolated and extraordinary. When those calls come, God is able to make them known to those to whom they come; but in the majority of cases He wants us to walk with Him in the common paths of Christian experience. This may be the best way of showing faith in Him. There are some who are always demanding the marvelous in their lives or they can not be satisfied. As Christians, let us present ourselves unto God, our intellect, judgment, reason, all our natural faculties, to be filled by His Spirit, and He will not permit us to take a wrong step in such practical matters as these.

**Had Paul reference to life insurance in 1 Timothy 5:8, and if so, will not the same teaching apply to lodge membership?**

I do not think Paul was referring to life insurance, since that is a modern institution and unknown in his day. But I think his words may be taken to commend certain forms of life insurance as a provision for our families after death. The same kind of a provision, for example, as a savings bank account. As to membership in a lodge, no Christian condemns that on the ground of its life insurance feature, but on the ground of its worldly associations, and antagonism to the real truth of the Gospel. I do not think the principle of life insurance shows a spirit of doubt as to God's promises to care for us, but I do think that membership in some lodges is fellowshiping with the world in a way that is displeasing to Him and harmful to the individual of whom it is true.

The correspondent quotes 2 Corinthians 6:14, 15, and I may say, that I think the text applies very aptly to joining a lodge, but not in the same sense to ordinary life insurance. We need to be careful to discern the things that differ (see margin of the Revised Version at Philippians 1:10).

### Does Revelation 13:15-18 refer to lodges?

I do not think it does refer primarily to lodges, but I am not surprised that some persons should seriously believe so. The secret-lodge system is not altogether bad by any means, that is, it has some features to which objection cannot be made, but as a system it has always seemed to me opposed to the spirit of the Gospel and to that of a free people. Christians would do well to keep out of it, and those who are in would do well not to stay in. The passage referred to in Revelation applies to the Antichrist who shall be revealed just prior to the coming of the Christ, but the antichristian principles out of which he will be evolved in that day have for a long time been operating in Christendom (2 Thessalonians 2), to which the secret-lodge system has contributed its full share. There is a close resemblance between some of its outbreathings and the words in Revelation.

### What do you think of secret orders?

These orders, as I understand it, do in a measure usurp the place of the church of Christ in professing to teach men their duty to God, themselves, and their fellowmen; for which they have priests, chaplains, altars, prayers and the Bible itself. But their prayers omit the name of Christ. This is calculated to mislead those who are not Christians, and persuade them that all the religion they need is found in the lodge. The system is also weakening to the faith of those who are Christians, throwing them into close association with the worldly-minded, weaning them from the prayer and testimony meeting, and absorbing money as well as time which belong more properly to the direct work of the Gospel. The charitable features of the lodge system have often been quoted in comparison with those of the church to the disparagement of the latter; but it is usually forgotten that the charity of the church is a gift bestowed where nothing is looked for in return, while that of the lodge is a *quid pro quo*, a kind of life insurance system where the man who gives is expected to be given to when his time comes. The young Christian will find it safer for him to be separated from these things.

**What is the meaning of Matthew 5:33-37, and on what ground can we justify the taking of even a judicial oath?**

The answer is that oath-taking in itself is not sinful. Jehovah swears by Himself, see Hebrews 6:13-18, also Isaiah 54:9. Jesus answered under oath to the high priest. The apostle Paul again and again calls upon God to witness. The prohibition in this case, therefore, must mean swearing in common intercourse and for frivolous reasons to which Jesus' countrymen were prone, and which is, alas! a sad offence in the present time.

Even children early fall into the habit of a mild form of swearing born of the example of their elders. Why should people commit the offence of saying, "O Lord!" "Great Heavens!" "Gracious!" "My Goodness!" "By Gosh!" "Gee!" What a list of these oaths there are! And how sinful!

**Has God ever founded any marriage system on earth?**

We should think so decidedly. Examine Genesis 2; Malachi 2:11-16; Matthew 19:3-9; 1 Corinthians 7; Ephesians 5:22-33; Hebrews 13:4; 1 Peter 3:1-7.

**What is the interpretation of Matthew 5:32 and 19:9, containing Christ's teachings on the subject of divorce?**

My understanding is, and I believe it is that of the Protestant church at large with few exceptions, that in the case of divorce on the ground of adultery, the innocent party is at liberty to marry again without committing sin in so doing. The Catholic church does not grant this privilege.

**Do the Scriptures teach that there were two kinds of wine in use, intoxicating and non-intoxicating? What is the consensus of Biblical scholarship along line? Did our Savior make intoxicating wine at the marriage feast, and did He use it in the institution of the Lord's Supper?**

This is an old question that will not down, and yet, like the Scriptural mode of church government or the meaning of the word "baptize," it is one on which Biblical scholars will differ doubtless to the end of time. The Bible itself does not positively settle the question, and hence men are inclined to settle it for themselves according to their early training, or prejudice, or their general judgment as to what it ought to be. It is, therefore, not safe ground on which to dogmatize.

There are several words translated "wine" in the Old Testament, the chief of which are "yayin" and "tirosh," and while both are sometimes used in the sense of non-intoxicating perhaps, yet the opposite is also true, and they are used when it is quite evident that intoxicating drink is being thought of. In the New Testament there are two words translated "wine," the one is "gleukos," which means a new, sweet wine, and is employed only in Acts 2:13, where clearly intoxicating properties are associated with it. The other is "oinos," which is sometimes used when intoxication is in mind, and sometimes where it is not necessary to draw that inference.

As to the consensus of Biblical scholarship on the question, there is no such thing, if by that is meant an unanimity of opinion. Volumes have been written on both sides, and will no doubt continue to be. I have always thought it was intoxicating wine Jesus made at the feast in Cana because the context seems to compel that view. As to the institution of the Lord's Supper, however, the case is different, because there it is not called wine, but "the fruit of the vine." This phrase may mean the expressed juice of the grape in an unfermented state as yet. There is some authority for saying that such was the character of the "wine" commonly used by the Jews at the Passover and if this be so, it goes far to establish the conclusion that such was the wine which Jesus used in instituting the supper at the close of that feast.

The correspondent who asks these questions speaks of advocates of high license in his town who are urging the alcoholic character of Bible wine as an argument in favor of the saloon. But surely there are enough arguments against the saloon to down it in the mind of every Christian, and right-thinking man, without touching this question at all. The whole trend of the Bible is against the saloon, against social-treating customs, against the manufacture and sale (except as poisons) of such stuff as now go under the names of wine, whiskey, beer and the like; and against even the private and moderate drinking of pure wines and liquors on the part of professed disciples of Christ, for reasons given very plainly in such passages as 1 Corinthians 8 and Romans 14. There are many things other than wine-drinking which may not be sins in themselves, but which become sins in certain circumstances, and surely this is to be said for everything associated with the saloon. How any Christian can deposit his vote for it is a mystery that will never be solved this side of the judgment day.

### Is it contrary to the Scriptures to eat pork? And what is the meaning of 1 Timothy 4:4?

I do not know that it is contrary to the Scriptures for Christians to eat pork, except as it is contrary thereto to eat anything that does not agree with us, and so unfits us to serve and glorify God in our bodies to the highest degree. Pork was forbidden the Jews in the Mosaic dispensation for ceremonial reasons chiefly, and yet for hygienic reasons also. What is good to be eaten by some people in some climates is not good for other people in other climates. This is largely a question for the individual to decide, perhaps under the advice of his physician. And yet people who see how hogs live are not strongly attracted to their flesh as a regular article of diet.

1 Timothy 4:4, to which the correspondent refers, is right in point here, and so is Titus 1:15 and Romans 14. The believer in Christ Jesus is not under the law in this sense, and is free to eat pork, if it agrees with him, giving God thanks.

### Does the Bible teach against the practice of modern hypnotism?

Very much depends on the inquirer's conception of "modern hypnotism." I have heard of some things which have gone under that name which the Bible decidedly teaches against (Deuteronomy 18:9-14). But I have heard of some other things which under the control of wise, upright and intelligent physicians might have real therapeutic value, and be much blessed in the removal of physical ill, without moral or spiritual harm to either patient or practitioner. But it is like some other things, alcohol, for example, unless it is handled with the utmost care and the most enlightened and conscientious regard for truth and rectitude it is a bane rather than a blessing. The average man had better keep away from it altogether until we learn more of what it is and does.

### What shall I do to restore friends who are carried away with Christian Science?

The best thing to do is to pray for them. The next best thing is to improve opportunities to set the truth before them, especially the truth about the blood of Christ atoning for sin. And the next, to lead a godly life as an example to them.

**Please explain James 4:1. When is war justifiable from a Christian standpoint?**

I am not sure that the words "wars and fightings" in that verse refer to national conflicts, and think that possibly James has in mind quarrels among individuals. At all events that war is justifiable on the part of Christian nations in the present time at least, admits of little question in my judgment. But this does not mean that it is justifiable for Christian nations to go to war against one another. And if they were really Christian they would not do so. War would seem to be justifiable to deliver the oppressed, to defend the right, to punish the wrong, but even so-called Christian nations very seldom, if ever, engage in war for these altruistic reasons. Such is their profession at times, but history reveals other motives that were more impelling. All this shows us what a hollow thing Christendom is, and substantiates and illustrates the teachings of Christ and the prophets concerning the course of the church and the world, and the necessity that Christ shall set up his kingdom on the earth at last through catastrophic judgments. See the books of Daniel and Revelation.

**Do you believe that a Christian is at liberty to vote, and if so, might he not be required, in case of riot or insurrection, to assist the government to put it down? In the latter case would he not by so doing, violate the command of our Savior, "I say unto you that ye resist not evil"?**

I believe not only that a Christian is at liberty to vote, but that ordinarily in this republic, it is his duty to do so. In the case of riot or insurrection should he be called upon by the government for aid, it would be his duty to respond, whether he voted or not. And this would not be a violation of the command of our Savior, because in the case quoted,

He was rebuking the Pharisees for perverting a just principle of God into a mere incitement to human revenge. We may not demand strict justice upon those who have done us a wrong individually, but that is not to say that we must remain passive in the presence of all evil, the consequence of which would be appalling. God Himself places the sword in the hand of the magistrate, and it is the duty of all good men to strengthen that hand.

**Please give your views concerning the tithe principle, which I do not feel quite sure ought to be insisted upon as binding in this dispensation. It has been suggested that we organize a voluntary tithers band in our church.**

I have never been able to see that the law of the tithe was harmonious to the Christian dispensation, and yet it is a sensitive matter to touch. It seems to me that the ground of appeal with reference to it is this: If under the law the people of God gave a tithe, how much more should they be willing to give under the Gospel? God looks upon the heart, and "If there be first a willing mind, it is accepted according to that a man hath, and not according to that he hath not." Unquestionably there are some Christians to whom the giving of a tenth would be a yoke greater than man should put upon them; while on the other hand a tithe for others is a very small affair. I do not think it would be wrong to "organize a voluntary tithers band" in your church, but to make it an obligation is another matter.

# CHAPTER VIII.

## QUESTIONS ON THE FUTURE LIFE.

A correspondent inquires the meaning of Ephesians 4:8, which speaks of Christ in His ascension as leading "captivity captive," and wishes to know whether the "captives" therein referred to were those who came up out of their graves at the time of His death and spoken of in Matthew 27:53.

It is quite evident that they include these, but there is another interpretation which makes the passage refer to all the saints who had died prior to the event spoken of, and whose abode had been in hades awaiting the moment of Christ's triumph, who then bore them with Him, as a conqueror his train, up to the place where He now is. Dr. Craven, the American editor of *Lange on Revelation*, elaborates this idea in his work on that book. The present writer refers to it more particularly in his *Progress in the Life to Come*.

**What is God's purpose in keeping a soul in misery, hopeless and useless through eternity, and how do you harmonize this with the character of God?**

First, it is not our business to harmonize this with the character of God. That is God's business. The same Bible that reveals God's character reveals the fact of the eternal conscious punishment of the wicked. Therefore, if we disregard its teachings in the one case, strict logic compels that we do it in the other. How do we know God's character except from the Bible? And if the Bible which tells us what His character is, tells us also that He will thus punish the wicked, what further harmonizing is necessary?

Secondly, there is a deeper and more inscrutable question

to solve than the one you ask; and if it were solved your question would be solved with it. We refer to the origin of evil. How can you harmonize that with the character of God? God is love, and yet He created this world and allowed sin to enter into it.

Thirdly, to go a little further, God's love includes justice; and justice in its very nature, demands the punishment of sin. A human government would go to pieces without it, and so would the divine government.

It is, however, the eternity of the retribution to which you refer especially, as to which you should remember that the punishment must continue as long as the sin continues. Jesus spoke of eternal sin (Mark 3:29, R. V.), and where there is eternal sin there must be eternal penalty. Further than this we cannot go, as the Bible affords no light beyond.

### Do the saved go immediately to heaven after death?

That is what I understand the Scripture to teach, though that does not mean that they are as yet in their condition of perfect felicity. This will not be till their bodies are raised from the dead, re-united to their souls, and glorified, at Christ's second coming.

### How would you interpret Matthew 12:31, 32, which says that blasphemy against the Holy Ghost shall not be forgiven, "neither in this world, neither in that which is to come"? Does it mean that there may be forgiveness in the world to come for other sins than this one?

Certainly not, for then the teaching would contradict the whole trend of Scripture. That trend is all in one direction, viz.: that man seals his future eternally by his acceptance or non-acceptance of Jesus in the present life. I think the simple and reasonable explanation is that of Dr. Broadus, that the words are merely a strong and extended declaration on the part of Jesus that this sin will never be forgiven. This interpretation is confirmed by the parallel passage in Mark, which declares that such an one is guilty of an eternal sin (R. V.).

**Why should there be any judgment day, inasmuch as God knows His sheep, who are lost and who are saved?**

A hint as to the answer is found in such scriptures as Psalm 51:4, Romans 3:19, 26 and Revelation 15:3. God is dealing with intelligent creatures in whose nature He has implanted the sense of justice and right, and from one point of view He Himself is on trial before them. The wicked now charge God with unfairness very often, and they must have an opportunity to see that beyond question this is not true. It is due to God that they should see this and confess it, and doubtless it will constitute part of their moral torment throughout eternity.

And in regard to the saved, we should remember that there is a judgment to determine the question of their fidelity to their Savior, with a distribution of rewards based upon it. Compare 2 Corinthians 5:10 and 1 Peter 1:17. This, too, involves a careful, complete, unbiased examination of motives as well as acts that will satisfy the subject of the judgment as well as the Judge, both of whom are to live together throughout eternity.

**Do you believe there will be a probation after death for the heathen who have died in ignorance and superstition?**

Romans 1:18-25 answers that question in part, by teaching that the heathen are responsible for their ignorance and superstition. They are not responsible perhaps for not knowing the historic Christ. We are responsible alas! for not sending them that knowledge. But they are responsible for their sin. And it is their sin for which they are condemned and not their ignorance of Christ. If any heathen, like Cornelius in Acts 10 and 11, lives fully up to the light he has, more light will be given him. I think we may take Cornelius' case as a kind of proof that Christ will be revealed to him. But our Christian missionaries meet very few cases like Cornelius.

### What do you understand by, "The soul that sinneth it shall die"?

I understand this to mean just what Romans 6:23, first half, means. "The wages of sin is death." Death, however, is not annihilation or non-existence but continued existence in a state of conscious eternal punishment. Christ bore the sins of the whole world when He died on the cross. He died on account of sin that they who believe on Him might not die. He was forsaken of God for a moment that we might not be forsaken forever. But this God-forsakenness is the lot of that man who dies in his sins. It is awful to contemplate. It makes the hand tremble to write the words. But unless men know the truth they will not fly for refuge to Him who is "the Way, the Truth and the Life."

### What is the meaning of 1 Peter 3:19, and why, if there is no salvation after death, should Christ have preached to the spirits in prison?

The word "preached" in that verse is not the usual one (in the Greek) used for preaching the Gospel. It means rather to "herald" or "proclaim" something, without saying just what. The "spirits in prison" in my present judgment, do not refer to the spirits of men, but angels; evil angels, of course, since they are "in prison." The particular evil angels in mind are those who were disobedient in Noah's day; see the following verse. If we wish to know the character of their disobedience, it is suggested in Genesis 6, in what is said about the "sons of God." The "sons of God" there refers not to men, I believe, but to angels, evil angels. They are the angels or "spirits in prison" to whom Christ heralded or proclaimed His triumph over them on the cross.

See verse 22 of the same chapter, also Colossians 2:15 and other places.

Allusion to these same "spirits in prison," and in somewhat similar connection, is made in 2 Peter 2:4, 5 and Jude 6, 7.

**Are you of the opinion that the passage, Matthew 27:52, 53, is true, and if so, why do not the other evangelists record so remarkable an occurrence?**

That the passage is true I have not the slightest doubt, because Biblical research testifies to its presence in all the versions and manuscripts from the first, and I am not aware that it has ever been questioned as to its authenticity. Why the other evangelists do not record it is as much of a mystery to me as to my correspondent, although it is qualified by the fact that many other marvelous things are chronicled by only one of the four. The Holy Spirit was pleased to have it so is the only answer I can give. These sleeping saints were Old Testament believers whose graves were opened by the earthquake at our Lord's death in preparation for their subsequent exit. This took place when the spirit of life from their risen Lord entered into them. Appearing to many in the city as they did, they were an undeniable evidence, not only of their own resurrection, but of His, and in all probability they ascended unto heaven with Him as trophies of His victory over death.

**What does Peter mean (1 Peter 4:6) by preaching to the dead? How "dead"?**

He means the Gospel was preached to them that are now dead while they were alive. It was not preached to them after they died, but while they were alive. The result is, that having accepted that Gospel, they now live before God in the spirit, even though while on earth they suffered as men in the flesh. The apostle is comforting and encouraging his Christian hearers passing through persecution by the example of Christ and that of some of their own number who had passed hence. Christ had been delivered and had triumphed. Some of their own number had likewise been delivered and had triumphed. They had been judged according to men in the flesh as Christ also had been judged. They now lived to God in the spirit as Christ also did. They were they who had had the Gospel preached to them while living.

### In what sense would some not taste of death till they saw the kingdom of God (Luke 9:27)?

In the sense illustrated by what followed this declaration of Jesus. Peter, James, and John saw the kingdom of God in embryo, or in miniature, and the glory of Christ, in His transfiguration. Compare 2 Peter 1:16-18.

### What is meant by being "baptized for the dead" (1 Corinthians 15:29)?

To quote the *Annotated Bible*, "Some find here an allusion to a practice (which was neither extensive or lasting) of baptizing persons in place of candidates who died before baptism," i. e., baptizing them as substitutes. Of course, if this view be taken, we must not suppose that Paul sanctions the practice, but simply uses it as an argument *ad hominem*, an argument against those who practiced it and yet denied the resurrection of the dead as some did in the Corinthian Church. How can they explain their action in baptizing for the dead if the dead do not rise again? This is what he seems to say.

But there are other explanations. Bengel, for example, translates it in a different way, suggesting that it applies to those who were baptized immediately before death. Many in the early church put off baptism till near death, why then should they take the trouble to be baptized at that moment if they would not rise again? Others regard the phrase as elliptical, meaning "baptized for the resurrection of the dead," this being one great object of their faith and hope. Finally, the word "baptized" has been taken figuratively, referring to the overwhelming trials which many suffered for the sake of their hope beyond death (Acts 23:6). The first of these explanations has always been sufficiently satisfying to me.

### What is conditional immortality?

Conditional immortality is an expression used to define a school of teaching which believes in the annihilation of the wicked, and that immortality or continued existence after death is "conditioned" upon our being in Christ. Only believers have immortality, they say. The opinion is unscriptural, I think. Immortality, or continued existence, seems to be conferred on all the spirits of men, but whether it will be a blessed immortality or the opposite is that which is conditioned on our being in Christ.

### What scriptures seem to teach that death is not annihilation or non-existence, but continued existence in a state of conscious eternal punishment?

Matthew 3:12; 5:29, 30; 8:12; 12:32; 13:42; 18:8, 9; 25:41, 46; 26:24; Mark 3:29; 8:36; 9:43-48; Luke 12:4, 5; 16:19-31; John 3:36; 5:29; 1 Thessalonians 1:10; 2 Thessalonians 1:8, 9; 1 Timothy 6:9; Hebrews 6:2; 10:26-31; 2 Peter 2:3-10, 17; 3:7; Revelation 14:10, 11; 19:20; 20:10, 15; 21:8.

A correspondent is in a quandary how to decide on the question of future retribution, as he finds students of the Word "equally honest and sincere," divided as to "whether future punishment is eternal, or whether all souls will come into harmony with God." He presents two inquiries, asking first, the opinion of the present writer, and secondly, how any person can come to a right decision in regard to it?

The opinion of the present writer is that the punishment is eternal. It almost paralyzes the hand to write it, or makes the tongue cleave to the roof of the mouth to speak it. But there seems to be no escape. The only way for a person to come to a right decision on the matter is prayerfully to study the Word of God. Personally, I feel almost persuaded that the students of the Word who say they do not find that truth there are simply seeking to deceive themselves. They do not want it to be there, and therefore refuse to look at it. They say also, that if others who do find it there really believed it, they would give up everything and spend the rest of their lives in telling people about it. Do they forget that One who did believe and who taught it, and the only religious teacher who did believe and teach it up until His day acted on that very principle, gave up all He had to tell people about it, and that they hanged Him to a tree?

The correspondent is asked to read the following scriptures. Matthew 10:28; 12:32; 18:8; 25:41; 25:46; 26:24; Mark 3:29 (R. V.); 9:43-48; Luke 3:17; 16:19-31; John 3:36; 5:29; Romans 6:23; 2 Thessalonians 1:9; Hebrews 6:2; 2 Peter 2:4-9, 17; Jude 6; Revelation 14:10, 11; 19:20, 21; 20:10; 20:15; 21:8.

There are two of these passages to which his attention is especially called, Mark 3:29 (R. V.) and Matthew 26:24. The first teaches that there is such a thing as "eternal sin," and hence, as a corollary, eternal punishment. The second, that Judas had better not have been born, which would not be the case if he should ever enter heaven.

Once when Jesus was asked by His disciples, "Are there few that be saved?" He did not reply, save by warning them to take heed to enter the straight gate. On another occasion He intimated that there would be some who would be beaten with many stripes, and others beaten with few, i. e., that there would be degrees or graduations of punishment (probably) in the next life. Besides these two hints, if one is pleased to call them so, there are no other qualifying utterances concerning this awful subject.

An inquirer asks two or three questions bearing on the application of the word "everlasting." He cites instances where it is used in a limited sense, i. e., other than in the sense of "forever and ever"; for instance, Canaan was given to the Jews for an "everlasting" possession (Genesis 17:8), and yet some day the earth is to be burned up (2 Peter 3:10).

Of course, in this case "everlasting" means only as long as the earth shall last, and there are other cases where the word has other time limits. But when the word is used with reference to the punishment of the wicked, time has passed out of the consideration altogether, and it is "everlasting," after time shall be no longer, everlasting without any kind of a limit known to our understandings. Indeed this word "everlasting" is the strongest word in the Greek language to express the idea of endlessness. It is that which Christ uses to express the thought of the blessing on the righteous (Matthew 25:46). See the Revised Version in this case, where the same word is used to describe the eternity of heaven and the eternity of hell.

It is the same word, too, which expresses the eternity of God, when He is called the "everlasting God." So while it is sometimes employed in the limited sense spoken of, it is also employed at other times where no limit can be placed upon it, and such would seem to be the case where future retribution is in view.

## Why do not the clergy preach more on the doctrine of future punishment?

The question is one which no one but the Searcher of Hearts can answer. Perhaps one reason is that the doctrine is so disagreeable to think about; another, that it is so hard to preach with tenderness; a third, that it is so stoutly resented by human nature; a fourth, that ministers as a class do not believe in it with the conviction of earlier days. It is true also, that many ministers conscientiously discount its value as a motive in turning men from sin in comparison with the presentation of the grace side of the Gospel. There is a deep-seated conviction in men that future punishment is certain and awful, and it is much harder to make them believe in and understand the meaning of divine grace through Jesus Christ.

But all this is not said in palliation of the neglect of preaching future punishment, which should be given its full place in "the due proportion of faith."

### Shall we know each other in the future life?

The writer has special reference to Jesus' words in Matthew 22:29, 30. I think that such passages as that in 1 Thessalonians 2:19 teach a recognition of one another in the future life which Christ's words referred to above do not contradict. The question of the Sadducees which Christ replied to on that occasion concerned whose wife the woman would be in the resurrection seeing she had had seven husbands. If there were no recognition in the resurrection it seems to me Christ would have answered this question by saying so. But as He says no such thing, but only that there will be no "marrying or giving in marriage" there the implication is that there will be recognition. The reason why there is no marriage in the resurrection is because there will then be no need for the reparation of losses by procreation. There will be no more deaths, and for that reason no more births will be necessary. But this does not involve the severance of all earthly ties beyond the grave.

A correspondent asks a number of question about the dead and the resurrection from the dead, some, if not all, of which may be answered without repeating the questions.

For example, the vision of the valley of dry bones in Ezekiel 37 is to be so regarded, i. e., as a vision, and not as an occurrence which actually took place. That is, the vision actually took place, it was something present to the mind of the prophet, but the valley, the dry bones, etc., were not real existences. The prophet intimates that it was a vision by saying, verse 1, that he was carried out "in the Spirit of the Lord."

The "Lazarus" whom Christ raised from the dead in John 11, is not the same as he who is named in Luke 16. The first was a real character who lived in Bethany. The second may have been only an imaginary person whom Christ used in telling the story.

When in Matthew 22:32, Jesus says, "God is not the God of the dead, but of the living," his words are explained in part by the comment given in the parallel place in Luke 20:38, which reads, "For all live unto him." "To God, no human being is dead, or ever will be, but all mankind sustain an abiding conscious relation to him," whether they are saved or lost, in heaven or hell. In this verse the special reference is, I believe, to the saved.

When in Acts 2:34 we read, "David is not ascended into the heavens," the reference is to his resurrection body. David was living as to his spirit, but his body was not yet raised from the dead and ascended, as in the case of Christ with whom he is being compared in the passage.

Though men die, so far as their physical part is concerned, they continue to exist as to their spiritual part whether with the righteous or the wicked dead. They are in a state of consciousness though not in that final state which will be theirs after the resurrection of their bodies.

All the dead will not be raised at the same time. The righteous dead arise when Jesus comes the second time (see 1 Thessalonians 4:16); but the rest of the dead will not rise till after the millennium, a thousand years later (see Revelation 20:1-6).

Those that arose from their graves at the time of Christ's death, doubtless went with Him to heaven at His ascension, but it is difficult to believe that they took those same bodies with them; doubtless they passed into the glorified state as they ascended. Unlike the son of the widow of Nain, Lazarus, and those referred to in 2 Kings 13:21, they will not die or be raised a second time.

How do you harmonize Paul's teaching in regard to the "spiritual body" in 1 Corinthians 15:44, and the "glorious body" in Philippians 3:21?

Shall our resurrection bodies be like Adam's in the age of innocence, or more glorious?

In regard to the "spiritual body" named in 1 Corinthians, the contrast is there being drawn between it and our natural body. This natural or "animal" body is one moulded in flesh and blood to suit the animal soul which predominates in it. The Holy Spirit, however, dwelling in believers on Jesus Christ, is an earnest, or pledge, or evidence of a superior state (see Romans 8:11-23), where He shall predominate and the animal soul be duly subordinate. When this takes place we shall have a spiritual body, one wholly moulded in other words, by the Spirit of God, and with an organism conformed to the higher and spiritual life (see 1 Corinthians 2:14; 1 Thessalonians 5:23). As Alford says: "It is no more wonderful a thing that there should be a body fitted to the capacities and wants of man's highest nature, than that there should be one fitted to those of his subordinate part."

As to the "glorious body" of Philippians 3:21, I think it means the same thing as the "spiritual body" we have just been speaking about. In other words, it identifies and photographs that body. Christ shall, through the Holy Spirit, transfigure the body in which our humiliation has place, that it may be conformed to the body of His glory, the body, that is, in which His own glory is manifested. He gave us a sample of this coming glorification or transfiguration on the mount (Matthew 17), in which we saw that it effected a change not in identity, but only in appearance and form. Jesus was the same Jesus on the Mount of Transfiguration as before, though His appearance was different. So our resurrection bodies as believers, since they shall be like His, shall be identical essentially with our present bodies.

As to a comparison with Adam's body before the fall, we can only say, that as we have no means of determining the appearance thereof, it is simply likely to be true that as the Second Adam is Himself more glorious than the first, so our likeness in Him is doubtless more glorious than that of the one whose sad work He came into the world to repair.

**Does Paradise in Luke 23:43; 2 Corinthians 12:4; and Revelation 2:7 have reference to the same place?**

I question whether it does, though no one can be certain. I believe that in every case it refers to a place of blessing for the true people of God, but that the location and conditions are different in each allusion to it. In the first instance, it refers to the location and condition of the righteous dead in the Old Testament dispensation; in the second instance, to their location and condition after the death, resurrection and ascension of Christ, which, I believe, may have been quite different (see such passages as Ephesians 4:8; John 14:1-3). In the third instance, it may refer to the location and conditions associated with the new heavens and the new earth of Revelation 21. The author's book entitled, *Progress in the Life to Come* might aid the correspondent to a better understanding of the subject.

# CHAPTER IX.

## QUESTIONS ON ISRAEL, OR THE JEWS.

Has the following promise made to Abraham been fulfilled: "In thy seed shall all the families of the earth be blessed" (Genesis 22:18)?

The seed of Abraham was, in the first instance, Isaac, and the nation of Israel that came from his loins through Jacob; but in the last instance, it is Christ, and those who believe on Him whether of national Israel or not (Galatians 3:29). One has only to reflect a moment to see how all families of the earth have already been blessed through Christ. The Gospel of the Son of God has been proclaimed in nearly every nation under heaven, and wherever it has gone it has brought salvation and blessing with it. Moreover, Jesus was a Jew, an Israelite of the Israelites, a descendant or seed of Abraham after the flesh, of whom Isaac was a type. And then, too, the nation of Israel, the seed of Abraham, was the depository for many centuries of the sacred oracles of God, and what a blessing have they been to all the families of the earth in that respect! It has been through the history of Israel that men have been taught the truth about Jehovah.

But all this refers to the past or the present, while the future holds still greater blessings for all the families of the earth through Israel, and especially in Christ who came from Israel after the flesh. All the blessings of the millennium on this earth come through Christ, the seed of Abraham, and will be manifested to the Gentile nations by means of Israel which, as a nation, will then be restored to her own land, and, what is still more important, will be restored to Jehovah through repentance and faith on Jesus as the Messiah. It is then that this original promise of Abraham will be fulfilled in a greater sense than has been yet realized.

**Is it a fact that all Jews, or all Israel, are going to be saved?**

Paul says (Romans 11:26): "All Israel shall be saved." But he does not mean by this every Israelite that ever lived. He is referring to the nation of Israel as it shall be existing on the earth in the day of which he speaks. This is the day of the return of our Lord and the ushering in of the millennium. It will be a sudden and miraculous occurrence brought about doubtless by the appearance of our Lord before them much as He manifested Himself to Saul en route to Damascus (Acts 9). See Zechariah 14:4; Revelations 1:7 and kindred scriptures.

**If we say that the Jews will be here, what scripture have we for thinking that they, as a nation, will be treated differently from all the rest of the human race at the coming of Christ.**

In reply, see Deuteronomy 30; Isaiah, chapters 11; 35; 40; 49; 51; 54; 60, etc.; Hosea 3; Amos 9:11-15; Micah 4; Zechariah, chapters 12-14; Romans 11. Besides these places, I would refer also to nearly the whole of the book of Psalms, and a large part of the book of Revelation.

We always need to remember, however, that the special treatment of the Jew, is not for the Jew's sake alone, not because he is so much preferable to the rest of human kind, not because God is partial in His kindness, but because it has pleased God in His purpose of blessing for the whole world, to use one nation as an instrument therein, and to choose Israel as that nation.

**Please give a definition of the abomination of desolation spoken of by Daniel as referred to in Daniel 9:23-27 and Matthew 24:15.**

I think it refers to an image of the Antichrist to be set

up as an object of worship in the temple at Jerusalem during the last week of years, that is, the last seven years of the present age. It will be coincident with the "great tribulation" on the Jewish nation and the second coming of Christ for their deliverance. There have been types or foreshadowings of this thing in earlier periods of Israel's history, as for example, when Antiochus Epiphanes polluted the temple, B. C. 170, and again when Jerusalem was besieged and the temple destroyed by the Romans under Titus, A. D. 70, but the ultimate and final application, or rather the real fulfillment of the prophecy I regard as pertaining to the future time specified.

**Please explain Psalm 35:5 and 6, which is difficult to harmonize with Christ's prayer in Luke 23:34.**

The key to these imprecatory psalms, of which the one cited is an example, is their millennial application. The writer is speaking as a prophet, and referring not so much to his own enemies as to the enemies of Israel and of God. These enemies are nations rather than individuals. He who writes is idealized as the personal representative of Israel oppressed by the Gentile nations of the world. The time is the end of the age when Israel is passing this her great tribulation, and the judgments invoked upon her enemies are the same as those uniformly referred to in the New Testament as falling on the Gentile nations at the second coming of Christ.

The correspondent sees no difficulty in harmonizing Matthew 25:41 or 2 Thessalonians 1:7-10, for example, with Luke 23:34, and for the same reason there need be none in the case of this or any of the imprecatory psalms. "The angel of the Lord" spoken of in the psalms is one of the Old Testament titles of Christ, and doubtless is to be so applied in this instance.

**How about the sale of land in Palestine? How are such transactions related to Jehovah's decree in Leviticus 25:23?**

The latter applied only to Israel's relationship to the land. Jehovah owns that land in a peculiar sense. He gave it to the children of Abraham forever, who were not at liberty to sell it in perpetuity. Nor have they ever sold it. They have been robbed of it by the Gentiles, and the Lord has permitted the robbery as a chastisement to them, but when their time of repentance and deliverance as a nation comes, the land will be restored to them. Jehovah will see to it that it is restored, for such is the teaching of all His prophets. The present sales and transfers are without warrant, and no clear title can be given to any buyer of a single foot of the land.

### Do you consider the Zionist movement a fulfillment of prophecy?

This movement is an effort on the part of an aggregation of well-to-do Jews to purchase Palestine from Turkey, if possible, and colonize their poor and distressed brethren in the land of their fathers. It is one of the signs of the times, pointing to the end of the age and the second coming of Christ. The prophets teach that the Jews will be in Jerusalem again in some kind of a national capacity when our Lord returns for their deliverance from their enemies, and also that they will still be unconverted so far as the acceptance of Jesus as their Messiah is concerned. With these teachings the movement of Zionism seems to harmonize; for if it prove successful, certainly a large number of Jews will thus return to Palestine, and that in an unconverted state, for these Zionists do not acknowledge Jesus as their Messiah, and for the most part are not influenced by any desire to fulfill prophecy. Their action is simply political and philanthropic.

At the same time, I do not say that the return of the Jews to Palestine under the auspices of Zionism is that generally referred to by the prophets. These speak of miraculous interpositions of Jehovah on behalf of Israel, and the eagerness of Gentiles to contribute to the movement. Perhaps a second and later migration is thus referred to by them. The thing for us to keep in mind is that the Jews are going back, and every movement in that direction, including this of Zionism, contributes toward the hastening of the end.

# CHAPTER X.

## QUESTIONS ON THE SECOND COMING OF CHRIST AND THE MILLENNIUM.

Do you believe in the secret rapture of the saints, and that Christ may come any moment?

Do you believe His church will pass through the great tribulation?

To whom does the Holy Ghost refer in Revelation 7:14? The one hundred and forty-four thousand, do they belong to the church?

Do the Old Testament saints belong to His church or will they form another company?

In reply to the first, I answer yes. In reply to the second, no. In reply to the third, Israel. In reply to the fourth, no, that is, I do not believe the Old Testament saints belong to the church, but are a company by themselves.

And yet the reader will please understand that these clear-cut responses necessitated by the limitation of space, are not put forth in a spirit of dogmatic positiveness. Brethren whose opinions I respect differ from me as to some of these questions of detail. But all students of prophecy are practically a unit on the one great fact that Christ is coming personally and visibly, and that his appearing antedates the millennium. The other matters are relatively unimportant.

Did Paul consider the possibility of Christ's return in his lifetime?

My judgment is that Paul did consider the possibility of the return of Christ in his day, just as we should do so in our day. But some one may say, "Then he was mistaken, and if so, how does that affect his inspiration?" But was he mistaken? Is there not a distinction between a mistake and a disappointment? I too, am looking for Christ in my day, and should He not come I shall be disappointed, but not mistaken, because, like Paul, I do not know just when He shall come.

Nor does Paul's mistake, even if it were such, affect his inspiration, because the latter attaches to his words and not his thoughts or opinions. There were matters in which Paul was mistaken other than this, but he frankly tells us so; and he was as truly inspired to tell us so as to tell us anything else whatsoever. What is to be contended for in the inspiration of the Scriptures is not inspired men but inspired writings. Whether the men, as to their thoughts, were right or wrong, the record of all things which they have given us is an inspired record. This is the Word of God.

**What will become of all that are not Christians at the second coming of Christ?**

It is difficult to answer that question. There are scriptures such as Matthew 24:36-51, 1 Thessalonians 5:1-3, 2 Thessalonians 1:6-10, 2 Peter 3:10-12, and Jude 14-16, which speak of terrific, devastating judgment. But there are other scriptures again which speak of a remnant being saved of Israel, and even a remnant from among the Gentile nations. We know, moreover, that the earth will be populously inhabited during the millennial reign. It would seem therefore, as though the judgments of that period while indeed vast in extent and awful in character, will be discriminating in some sense, and not result in total destruction. Those very judgments may result in the repentance and conversion of many who, if not joined to the church or body of Christ, will nevertheless be saved.

**Please explain the words of Jesus in Matthew 24:34, Mark 13:30, and Luke 21:32, where He says, "This**

generation shall not pass till all these things be fulfilled.''

"These things" include events to synchronize with His second coming, and hence the mystery. Some would say, however, that all these things were fulfilled in the destruction of Jerusalem by the Romans, A. D. 70, which would entirely do away with the mystery. My opinion is contrary to this, however, and I am inclined to take the word "generation" in the sense of "race." This race, i. e., the Jews as a distinctive people, shall not pass away till these things be fulfilled.

A correspondent is troubled on a question of interpretation touching the judgment on the living nations spoken of by Christ in Matthew 25. The one class enters upon eternal life, while the other is cast in eternal punishment. The question is, How can nations, as such, be eternally punished?

We can not conceive of them existing as nations in eternal punishment, and if we say that such punishment for them means only that they go into non-existence as nations, then we encourage a similar application of that word punishment to the wicked individual soul.

The answer would seem to be that, while the time of this judgment is at the end of the present age when Jesus comes, and its scene the present earth, and its subject the living Gentile nations, that nevertheless the punishment must be individual. A moment's reflection will satisfy us as to this. If a nation is blessed it only becomes conscious of its blessing in the lives of its individual citizens, and the same thing must be true if instead of blessing it receive cursing.

Who first taught in the church that the saints would not pass through the tribulation and that the translation of the church might come to pass any time?

The correspondent always understood this doctrine to be

the primitive faith, he says, but has recently seen it stated that such a belief was unknown before the days of Edward Irving.

My own understanding of the subject agrees with that of the correspondent, having always believed that to Jesus Christ Himself and the inspired apostles, not Edward Irving, we were indebted for that comforting truth.

The late F. L. Chapell, D. D., has some very practical thoughts along this line of the church and the tribulation, some of which, because of the broad interest in the subject, I feel led to use. Of course, there is a sense in which the church is in tribulation of some sort as long as she is in the world, a tribulation which is likely to increase to sharp persecution as the end of the age draws near, but that is not "the great tribulation" mentioned, for example, in Daniel 12:1; Revelation 7:14 and other places, and to which the correspondent particularly refers.

This great tribulation is one of judgment, it has distinctively Jewish aspects, it includes every horror, and men grow blasphemous and God-defying under it, which is quite a different result from what we would expect of a disciplinary experience of the church.

This at once raises the question as to what is meant by the "church," which some think will pass through the tribulation. It can hardly be the true, pure church, as Dr. Chapell thinks, because those who belong to her are exhorted "to so live that they may escape all these things," but it may indeed be the nominal, worldly, slumbering church.

The lesson of it all is, that if we separate ourselves from the world we shall suffer tribulation, but it will be the tribulation of discipline. If we mingle with the world we may escape the tribulation of discipline, but shall fall into that of judgment.

**If all the believers, living and dead, are caught up at the rapture (1 Thessalonians 4:17), and all the unbelievers punished with everlasting destruction at the**

revelation (2 Thessalonians 1:9), who are left to people the earth during the millennium?

The inquirer must see at once that there is a fault in his exegesis somewhere. Perhaps it will aid him to remember that some time elapses, we know not how long, between the rapture and revelation. Also, that the rapture itself may bring many unbelievers to their senses when they will come to know God and obey the Gospel of Jesus Christ. Furthermore, throughout the prophetic teachings of both testaments, the nations referred to as being visited with Christ's judgments when He comes are those of Christendom, the nations forming the old Roman Empire, leaving out of view to a certain extent what we now know as heathendom. Finally, in that picture of His judgments on the living nations given in Matthew 25, which takes place after the rapture as it would seem, and which synchronizes with the one referred to in 2 Thessalonians, there are some to be placed on His right hand and to inherit the kingdom. The ground for the discrimination there, however, is a peculiar one, viz.: Their treatment of Christ's brethren after the flesh, i. e., Israel.

It looks, therefore, as if the nations were to have a chance to show fealty to Him by ministering to Israel, perhaps in restoring them to their own land again after the rapture, before these final destructive judgments fall. We must keep in mind that the Day of the Lord, which is the period to which Paul is referring in 2 Thessalonians rather than the single event of Christ's coming for His church, is a long day, and one in which there will be time for the culmination of a great many events spoken of by the prophets. Confusion of thought now will give way to clearer vision as the time approaches.

It might indeed be added as a supplementary thought, that Alford interprets the latter clause of verse 9, thus: "Driven from the manifestations of His power in the glorification of His saints." To be thus cast out from the presence of the

Lord is the idea at the root of eternal death, it is evil left to its own working, but it may be some time before the full result of that working is experienced and realized. The unbelieving may be cast out, i. e., from the presence of Christ's glory, but yet remain to some extent upon the earth.

**Will Christ's mediatorial reign extend to the heathen who died ignorant of the atonement, and to such others as were deceived by false teaching, in the millennial or any other reign?**

I could answer this question more intelligently if I were sure of the writer's understanding of "Christ's mediatorial reign." I imagine he means that perfect reign of Christ as Mediator which will probably follow the millennial age, and yet, after all, no matter what he means by it, perhaps the answer to his inquiry should, as to the main point, be still the same. As I understand the Scriptures, there is no hope for any man in this or any previous age who dies, or has died, in his sins. I doubt if false teaching will have any place in the millennial age, although men, even in that age, will doubtless die unreconciled to God. But if they so die, I know no scripture which gives us reason to believe they will have another chance in any other age or reign, if that is what the correspondent means. On the contrary, the analogy of other ages is all against it.

**An inquirer asks several questions which may be summed up under the one title of "Physical Conditions in the Millennium."**

I may say, in reply, that the present age is not to end by the depopulation of the earth in the great tribulation; that births and deaths will doubtless occur in the millennial age as now only under holier and happier conditions, that the unoccupied and unsubjugated territory of the earth will then be utilized by the people with an ease, and to an advantage, hardly dreamed of at the present time; and that the church will remain with the Lord in the air, and not descend upon, in the sense of inhabitating, the earth.

As to this last point, I believe the glory of the church with her Lord in the air will be a manifested glory, a glory which will be seen and recognized by the earthly saints of that period. I believe, too, that there will be a communication between the glorified church and the earthly saints of which at the present time we can know but little, but I do not think the glorified church will be located on the soil.

The correspondent has been confused by allusions to the coming of Christ *for* His church, and the coming of Christ *with* His church. Neither means that during the millennium Christ and His church will abide on the crust of the earth. It is indeed said, in Zechariah, that "His feet shall stand upon the Mount of Olives," a prophecy to be literally fulfilled, no doubt; but this has reference, I think, to His special appearing to Israel and for their deliverance at the time of their great tribulation. It is said that: "He shall sit upon the throne of his father David," and this, too, shall be fulfilled in that He shall reign as the recognized King of Israel; but it is just as possible for Him to do this from His position with His church in the air, and by means of an earthly vice-regent, as it is for King George to reign over India from his place in Buckingham palace, by means of his viceroy.

We are to remember that such Scriptural phrases as "the day of the Lord," the "coming of the Lord," etc., are to be understood as referring to events of several aspects and covering much time, practically the whole of the millennial period. We are to remember also the physical fact, that the "clouds" and the "air" so often referred to in connection with these events are really part of the earth, though not that part of it which men in the flesh inhabit.

Touching the physical conditions of the millennium, the correspondent would be aided by reading Isaiah 11, and kindred passages of Scripture to which he would be referred by the marginal references.

**Referring to 2 Thessalonians 2:3, what is meant by the "falling away," and who is meant by the "man of sin," or "son of perdition"?**

The "falling away" refers to an apostasy in the church, a falling away from the truth of the Gospel on the part of the professing people of God, a defection from the faith in Christendom. The "man of sin" is an individual who particularly represents that defection; or in whom that apostasy may be said to be headed up or incarnated. Many have thought Roman Catholicism to be intended by the "falling away," and the Pope to be the "man of sin," otherwise known as the Antichrist. But the trend of prophetic scholarship is more and more away from that view. For however Roman Catholicism may contribute to the apostasy, and however the history of the popes may foreshadow the Antichrist, the apostasy is greater and deeper than the one, and the Antichrist greater and wickeder than the other.

It is incumbent on us to face the fact that there is a falling away in Protestantism as serious, or even more so, than that in Romanism. The denial of the integrity of the Scriptures, the incarnation and deity of Christ, and atonement only through His shed blood, is peculiar to Protestantism and not Romanism, and it is more serious in its nature than mariolatry and priestism combined. It is the destructive Biblical criticism of these times that is giving encouragement to the anarchism and godless socialism that menaces government with an awful menace; and when its stability is undermined, that despot will arise, a kind of successor of Nebuchadnezzar, who will rule things with an iron hand, and in the power of Satan. Blaspheming the Name of God, and persecuting His saints, he will merit the full description of the "man of sin."

# CHAPTER XI.

## QUESTIONS ON SATAN, ANGELOLOGY AND MODERN "ISMS."

**Please explain 1 Samuel 16:14, which speaks of "an evil spirit from Jehovah" coming upon Saul. How did it come from Jehovah?**

Of course it came in the way of judgment. God has control in the last analysis, of all spirits, good and evil, human and angelic, and He may use them as He will, or give them liberty to act in certain cases as He sees fit. Take the case of Job as an illustration. That Satan himself had some kind of access to God is there apparent, and God undoubtedly gave him certain limited power over His servant Job. If He did that to test a true servant may He not do that to punish a wicked one? Of course, some would explain this away altogether, by saying that it was not really an evil spirit that troubled him, but his own gloomy reflections at this time that produced a morbid melancholy, but it is not wise to take such liberties with the sacred text, and in the present instance I see no necessity to do so.

**(1) Was Satan created by God? (2) If so, was he holy or sinful when created? (3) If sin entered when Satan fell was sin created, if so how, and by whom? (4) Did Adam, when created, have any sinful tendencies?**

I reply, (1) Satan was a creation of God. (2) He was holy when created. (3) The origin of sin is unknown further than it is revealed in the Bible. Satan was a fallen creature when he approached our first parents, but how he fell is only hinted at. It was through pride, Paul says, and doubtless expressed itself in a desire to grasp at the Godhead (1 Timothy 3:6; Philippians 2:5, 6), but how sin could have entered into a holy being is the mystery. (4) Adam had no sinful tendencies when created.

### When did "Satan as lightning fall from heaven"?

I am not aware that any definite answer can be given. There are several critical periods in the past that might be named, and yet there is reason to think Christ spoke prophetically, and that the time is co-incident with His second coming as indicated in Revelation 20.

### Had Satan power by his own possession or ownership to give Christ the kingdoms of the earth?

At first, one is inclined to say "No," because it seems so unreasonable to our limited understandings, and because Satan is a liar and deceiver. But on the other hand, the Holy Scriptures assign great power and even dignity of a certain kind to Satan. He has had access to God as we see from the book of Job. He is called the god of this world, the prince of the power, or powers, of the air. The book of Revelation gives us many evidences of the great place he holds in the affairs of nations and of men. On the whole, I am strongly inclined to think there was some sense or degree in which Satan was able to deliver what he promised. It seems almost necessary to believe this to give to the temptation of Jesus its real character. More over, there is nothing in the reply of Jesus to the tempter leading us to feel that he regarded the claim of Satan other than genuine. Indeed, the very opposite is the case. If Satan had been making a profession in that matter altogether untrue, how very different one would think our Lord's answer would have been. Yes, there was some kind of a deputed supremacy which Satan had and which he was able to turn over to our Lord.

### Does Satan speak the truth or a lie when, in Luke

### 4:6, he says the kingdoms of this world have been delivered unto him?

He speaks a half-truth. Thrice does our Lord call him "the prince of this world," and the inspired apostle Paul calls him "the god of this world" (2 Corinthians 4:4), all of which is not hyperbole or figurative speech, but possesses a basis of fact. Satan even has the power of death (Hebrews 2:14). Of course, it can be said that these references express only men's voluntary subjection to the rule of Satan, and even this is a real and terrible sway of power, but in my opinion they express more. It has always seemed to me as if this earth and its rule may have been committed unto Satan at the beginning and before his fall, and that he has not been entirely denuded of his power even yet. Men make a mistake to laugh at and belittle Satan.

### In what sense does Jehovah create evil, Isaiah 45:7?

That the reference is not to moral evil, that is, to sin, is evident from James 1:13. It means war, disaster, plagues, etc., in contrast to peace, and quietness and blessing, as the context shows. Jehovah, through the prophet, is at this time contrasting Persia with Babylon, Cyrus with Nebuchadnezzar, and He purposes to give prosperity to the one and calamity to the other. The Persians, represented by Cyrus, believed in two co-existent, eternal principles, ever struggling with each other, light and darkness, or good and evil. Ormuzd was the name of one god, and Ahriman of the other. But Jehovah here asserts His sovereignty over both. It is He who does these things, creating light and darkness, good and evil, i. e., giving blessing in one place and the judgment or cursing in another.

### What is the significance of the phrase "sons of God" in Genesis 6:2; Job 1:6 and 38:7?

I believe it refers to the angels. But the context must determine whether good or evil angels are meant. In the first instance the reference seems to be to evil angels, and in the other two, certainly in the last, to good angels. The evil angels, I should say, were the same in character and relationship as those mentioned in Revelation 12:9, to which the inquirer refers.

A correspondent inquires if the "sons of God" (Job 38:7) were inhabitants of earth or heaven?

I should say, heaven.

The writer also wishes to know if they are the same "sons of God" who intermarried with Seth's descendants (Genesis 6:2)? They are the same, I think, as to their nature or the class of beings to which they belong, but they are not necessarily the same individual beings. The "sons of God" is a phrase used in the Old Testament of angels, but the context must determine whether good or evil angels are meant. Job 38:7 seems to refer to the one class, and Genesis 6:2 to the other.

He asks further: "Are they the devil's angels cast out as in Revelation 12:9?" I should say those spoken of in Genesis 6:2 belonged to the same class of evil angels though not necessarily the same particular beings. Those spoken of in Genesis 6:2 seem to be referred to again in 2 Peter 2:4 and Jude 6.

**Please give an explanation of the circumstance that although David had served Saul as indicated in 1 Samuel 16:19-23, yet Saul did not recognize him afterwards as shown in the following chapter, verse 58.**

This, let me say, is one of the incidental evidences of the truth of the Bible. Frauds and imposters, in preparing such a work would have been too wary to have left such an apparent discrepancy exposed. The Bible, however, not fearing the light, leaves us to such reasonable explanations as the following: (a) Some time, perhaps, some years, may have elapsed between chapters 16 and 17, bringing marked changes in the appearance of a young lad like David. (b) Saul confessedly was under the power of a disordered brain, accounting for his inability to recognize one who had waited upon him when these Satanic delusions were in control. (c) Saul may not have been totally unacquainted with David, but the youth had now sprung into such great prominence as the result of his victory over Goliath, that the little Saul had known of him theretofore seemed inadequate to account for what now appeared. This last is the view of Fairbairn.

### How was David "a man after God's own heart"?

Not in the sense that he was not a sinner, of course, but in the sense that notwithstanding his sin, down in the bottom of his heart he loved God supremely. The governing motive of his life was to know the will of God and do it. No better illustration and proof of this could be asked than that found in a comparison of his life, step by step, with that of Saul, his predecessor on the throne, and his contemporary in history. They were both sinners, but one was ever self-justifying, the other self-condemning.

### Why are not more of the "Pentecost" people in control of demons after the manner of the "Tongues" movement?

The "Pentecost" people is a generic term that needs specialization. They are not all thoughtless, excitable fanatics. Some are sober students of the Word of God even though they may be mistaken in some points, or disagree with the inquirer, or with us. I have known some thus classed with whom one might have had much fellowship. But any Christian may fall under the control of demons, who, because of sin, or a weak mind, or an uninstructed heart, yields himself to spiritual influences that are not of God. It is dangerous to be seeking the marvelous and spectacular in our Christian experience. If we remember that as believers on Christ Jesus we are already baptized by the Holy Spirit into His body, it will save us from many extravagances.

### What is this new cult of Bahaism?

In one of its own publications, Sprague's *Story of the Bahai Movement*, it is referred to as "the latest expression of an eclectic evolution, growing out of the innate pantheism of the Iranian mind."

Pantheism is the doctrine that there is no personal God, only an impersonal divine essence out of which all things are evolved, first the mineral, then the plant, then the animal, and finally man. In every age this impersonal essence finds expression in some individual man, who, to all intents and purposes, is the god of that age.

Bab was the founder of this movement in 1850. After his death, Suth-i-Ezel became the head of the sect, whose brother-in-law, Baha, entrusted by him with its secrets, vaulted into the place of power through the role of assassin. It is from him the sect takes its name. "Our God, El Abha," "The Everlasting Father," are among the names applied to him. He died in 1892, in Acre, Syria, and his place is now taken by his son, Abdul Baha.

The sect is finding its way into Great Britain and the United States, and is one of the many anti-Christian movements of these times, deluding men and blinding their eyes to "the true light which lighteth every man that cometh into the world."

### Who was Ritschl and what is Ritschlianism?

For some purposes it is sufficient to say that Ritschl and Ritschlianism, stand for a distinct school of theology, originating in the last century, and which represents an old heresy under a new name; but Dr. Edward H. Merrell in a recent number of *The Bible Student and Teacher*, gives a sketch of the teaching of this school and its founder from which the following is quoted:

"Albrecht Ritschl has the reputation of being a good man. He was born in 1822 and died as a professor at Göttingen in 1889. He sat at the feet of many of the great theologians, absorbing their conflicting theories, but although he touched all phases of the theological thought of his time, he brought all to the test of his own intelligence, employing the method of the so-called 'value-judging,' a distinctive characteristic of his school of thought.

"Ritschlianism teaches that we have a positive and personal revelation from God, whose fulness is found in the unique person Jesus Christ. Through Christ we have the knowledge of the character and will of God, of the nature of the kingdom He is establishing in the earth, and of the motives needed to lead souls to become organic in that kingdom. It holds that through Christ all religion has had historical realization in the midst of the kingdoms of this world.

"But, strange to say, while Ritschlianism believes in the historical Christ, it holds neither to His incarnation nor bodily resurrection. It distinctly teaches that we have a sinless Christ, and yet, as Professor Orr phrases it, 'The pre-existence of Christ is cut off at one end and His exaltation and heavenly reign at the other.'"

### May the word "create" in Genesis 1 be interpreted in the sense of the evolutionary theory?

No. The Hebrew verb "bara" translated "create" in Genesis 1 carries with it in this instance the meaning of creation out of nothing. Not that it always and necessarily means that, but that it possesses such a meaning here. This is evident because it is used in such a discriminating way. It occurs three times in the chapter, for example, in verse 1 at the introduction of life in the fifth day, and the creation of man in the sixth day. Elsewhere, when only transformations are meant, as in the second and fourth days, or a continuation of the same kind of creation, as in the land animals of the fifth day, another word is used, "asah," translated "made." "Bara" is thus reserved for marking the first introduction of each of the three great spheres of existence—the world of matter, the world of animal life and the world of spirit as represented by man, all three of which, though intimately associated, are profoundly distinct in essence, and together constitute all the universe known to us. Professor Guyot, the distinguished scientist of France and the United States, from whom the previous sentence is taken, adds also that wherever the simple form of "bara" is used in the Bible, it is always with reference to a work made by God, and never by man. These considerations, with others, justify the foregoing definition of "creation."

### Were the higher forms of life developed from the lower forms?

The original creation of matter, the creation of the system of life, and the creation of man are three distinct creations out of nothing. "They are not simultaneous, but successive, and God's action in them is constant"; therefore, evolution from one into the other, from matter into life, or animal life into spiritual life is impossible. Great thinkers, who are at the same time devout men, are willing to admit that there may be evolution within any one or each of these systems considered by itself; i. e., matter may evolve itself into various forms of matter, and animal life into various forms of animal life, and human life into various forms of human life; but this is different, even if proven to be true, from that other kind of evolution which would make man the descendant of an ape and drive God out of the universe He has made. To the above it may be added that to the great Agassiz development, meant development of plan as experienced in structure, not the change of one structure into another. To his apprehensions the change was based upon intellectual not material causes. See his life, Vol. 1, pp. 244-245.

## SUBJECT INDEX

Abraham—God's promise to....104
"Abomination of desolation"..105
Adam and spiritual death, 56; when created, did he have sinful tendencies? 117.
Adam nature ..................... 65
Amalekites ........................ 27
Anger justified .................. 77
Ascension of Jesus Christ...... 35
Assurance of new birth........ 55
Atonement ....................... 53

Bahaism ........................121
Baptism, 71; of Jesus, 31; of Holy Ghost, 66; for the dead, 96; and salvation, 72.
Believing on Christ............. 54
Blasphemy against the Holy Ghost ........................... 92
Bible—Canon of N. T., 9; Authenticity of, 9; Is it the same as Apostles had? 10; Inspiration of, 11; Supposed contradictions of, 11; Synthetic study of, 16; Other methods of study, 19; What version preferred? 22.
Brotherhood of man............. 24

Canon of New Testament...... 9
Children dying before age of accountability .................. 59
Christian, The—His relation to Christ's ascension, 35; Shall he entertain unbelieving friends and strangers? 49; His obligation, 76; His vote, 89.
Christian ministry—its orders.. 48
Christian Science ............... 88
Church, The—Is it the body of Christ, and also His bride? 38; Withdrawing from, 39; Why do not men attend? 40; Raising money for support, 43; Scripture warrant for institutional features, 44; and laboring man, 46.
Conditional immortality ........ 97
Contemporaneous writers who mention Jesus Christ and His resurrection ............... 33
Contradictions in the Bible.... 11

David serving Saul, 120; a man after God's own heart, 121.
Dead, Baptism for the.......... 96
Death—Not annihilation or non-existence, 97; Not tasting of, 96; of the soul, 94.
Denominationalism ............. 45
Divine healing .................. 73
Divorce, Christ's teachings on 85

Election ........................... 63
Eradication of sin............... 62
Esau rejected, Jacob chosen... 60
"Everlasting"—what it means.. 93
Evil spirit from Jehovah...... 117
Evolution ........................123

Fairs, socials, etc., in the church ........................... 44
Faith or repentance: which is experienced first? ............. 61
"Falling away" .................116
Fatherhood of God, 23; and brotherhood of man, 24.
Feet-washing .................... 42
Future punishment ............. 99
Future retribution ............. 97

Gifts of the Spirit............... 73
"Glorious body" ................102
God—The Father, at Jesus' baptism, 23; May the unbeliever call Him Father? 23; Fatherhood of, 23; Holy Spirit called God, 28; His command to destroy the Amalekites, 27; How He "elects," 27; Does He repent? 26; Hardening Pharoah's heart, 26; Merciful to whom He will, 69; His "inheritance in the saints," 70; instituted marriage, 85; Character of, 91; Promise to Abraham, 104; In what sense did He create evil? 119.
Gospel—why "good news"?.... 57

## Subject Index

Harnock and *What is Christianity?* .......................... 24
Heathen—Destiny of, without Christ .......................... 59
Heaven ..................92, 101, 103
Holiness .......................... 62
Holy Spirit—Does He endow all Christians with an understanding of the Word? 21; at the baptism of Jesus, 23; is God, 28; Best books on subject of, 28; Blasphemy against, 92.
Hypnotism .......................... 88

Imprecatory passages ..........106
Infants and their salvation..58, 59
Inspiration of the Bible........ 11
Institutional church .......... 44
Intercession of Jesus............ 75

Jehovah of O. T., how related to Jesus of N. T. .............. 36
Jesus Christ—Main article in His message, 25; Date of birth, 29; Under what "law" made (or born), 29; Did He have help from God before twelve that other children do not have? 31; Manner of His baptism, 31; His temptation, 32; Transfiguration of, 32; Could He have saved Himself from the cross? 32; Resurrection of, 33, 34; Where was His soul while body lay in grave? 34; Is His body now the same as when resurrected? 35; His ascension, 35; His material blood in heaven? 35; Relationship to Jehovah of Old Testament, 36; The "Name above every name," 36; His body and bride, 38; His charge to Peter, 39; His command to wash disciples' feet, 42; If He can save all, why are not all saved? 56; His intercession, 75; made wine, 86; "Leading captivity captive," 91; Preaching to the spirits in prison, 94; His anticipated return during Paul's lifetime, 109; His mediatorial reign, 114.
Jews—all to be saved? 105; How treated at Christ's coming? 105.
Judgment day .................... 93
Judgment of living nations....111
Justification and sanctification. 62

Kingdom of heaven.............. 38

Laboring man and the church 46
"Lawful use of the law"...... 69
"Leading captivity captive".... 91
Life insurance ................82, 83
Lodge membership ............83, 84
Lord's Supper and human ordination ........................ 49

"Man of sin" ....................116
Mark of the beast.............. 80
Marriage instituted by God.... 85
Men in the church.............. 40
Millennium, Who on earth during, 112; Physical conditions during, 114.
Ministers ........................ 48
Miracle-working in the present age ............................. 74
Modern researches in Bible lands ............................ 14

"Name above every name"...... 36
Nativity, Date of................ 29
New Testament—Canon of, 9; Its teaching on second work of grace and baptism of Holy Ghost, 65, 66.

Oath-taking ...................... 85
Old heart with new nature, or new heart? .................... 25
Old Testament believers.58, 95, 109
"Once in grace, always in grace"? .......................... 63
Orders in the Christian ministry ............................ 48
Ordination as a prerequisite to ministry of the Lord's Supper 49

Palestine, Sale of land in......106
Paradise ........................103
Passion Play .................... 47
Paul on Mars Hill, 24; His view concerning woman, 41; When and where sanctified? 62; Christ's anticipated return during his life-time, 109.
"Pentecost" people and demons ............................121
"Perfect"—its two-fold use..... 65
Peter charged by Christ........ 39
Pharoah's heart hardened...... 26
Pork-eating ...................... 87
Prayers properly addressed to whom? .......................... 75
Preaching of the Gospel, with signs and miracles............ 74
Preaching, to the dead, 95; on future punishment, 99.
Probation after death.......... 93

## Subject Index

Rapture of the saints............109
Recognition in the future life..100
Regeneration .................... 61
Rejection of Christ.............. 64
Resurrection body, Character of ..............................102
Resurrection of Jesus Christ, 33, 34; How long in grave? 34; Where was His soul while body lay in grave? 34.
Ritschl and Ritschlianism......122
Rosetta Stone .................... 14

Sabbath observance ..........78, 79
Salvation and infants........58, 59
Sanctification ................62, 65
Satan—His right to offer Christ the kingdom of the earth, 118; Created by God? 117; his fall from heaven, 118.
"Scapegoat" defined ............ 54
Second work of grace........... 65
Secret orders ................83, 84
Sermons, written or extempore? 51
Seventh-Day Adventism......80, 81
Sin—Unpardonable, 67; "Not unto death," 67; How it entered the world, 117.
"Sons of God"....................119
"Son of perdition."..............116
"Soul" and "spirit" distinguished ........................ 53
Spirits in prison................. 94
"Spiritual body" ...............102

Temptation of Jesus............ 32
Tithing .......................... 90
Transfiguration of Jesus........ 32
Translation of the church......111
Tribulation and the church....109
Trinity .......................... 75

Unbelievers—shall they be received by Christians for the discussion of anti-Christian ideas? 49; at Christ's coming, 110.
Union with Christ............... 71
Unitarian, The, how to deal with him ............................ 56
Unpardonable sin .............. 67
Usury ........................... 81

Verbal inspiration of the Bible 11
Victory over sin..............25, 66
Voting ........................... 89

War justifiable? ................. 89
Wine in the Bible............... 86
Woman, Paul's views concerning ............................. 41
Worldly amusement and the regenerated soul ................. 61

Zionist movement ..............107

# INDEX TO BIBLE TEXTS

## GENESIS
1 .....................123
2:7 .................... 53
3:17 ................... 56
6:3 ...................119
17:8 ................... 99
22:18 .................104

## EXODUS
33:19 .................. 69

## LEVITICUS
16 ..................... 54
25:23 .................106

## 1 SAMUEL
15:13 .................. 27
16:14 .................117
16:19-23 ..............120

## JOB
1:6 ...................119
38:7 ..................119

## PSALMS
16:5 ................... 81
35:5, 6 ...............106
51:4 ................... 98

## ISAIAH
7:14-16 ................ 30
45:7 ..................119

## JEREMIAH
31:22 .................. 30

## EZEKIEL
37 ....................100

## DANIEL
9:23-27 ...............105

## MATTHEW
5:32 ................... 85
5:33-37 ................ 85
12:31, 32 .............. 92
16:18 .................. 39
18:10 .................. 59
19:9 ................... 85
22:29, 30 .............100
22:32 .................101
24:15 .................105
24:34 .................110
27:52, 53 .........91, 95
28:1 ................... 33

## MARK
13:20 .................110
16:1 ................... 33
16:14-16 ............... 75
16:17, 18 .............. 74

## LUKE
4:6 ...................119
9:27 ................... 96
18:16 .................. 59
20:38 .................101
21:32 .................110
23:34 .................106
23:43 ............34, 103
24:1 ................... 33

## JOHN
6:44 ................... 23
8:41 ................... 23
20:1 ................... 33
20:17 .................. 34
20:23 .................. 39

## ACTS
2:27 ................... 34
2:34 ..................101
5:36 ................... 13

## ROMANS
3:19, 26 ............... 93
5:13 ................... 57
6:3, 4 ................. 72
6:4 .................... 71
6:23 ................... 94
8:34 ................... 75
9:15 ................... 69
11:26 .................105

## 1 CORINTHIANS
8:6 .................... 23
11:5 ................... 41
12:8-11 ................ 73
14:34, 35 .............. 41
15:29 .................. 96
15:44 .................102

## 2 CORINTHIANS
6:14 ................... 39
12:4 ..................103

## EPHESIANS
1:13 ................... 70
4:5 .................... 71
4:6 .................... 23
4:8 .................... 91
4:26 ................... 77

## PHILIPPIANS
2:9 .................... 36
3:12, 15 ............... 65
3:21 ..................102

## COLOSSIANS
1:23 ................... 21

## 1 THESSALONIANS
2:19 ..................100
4:17 ..................113

## 2 THESSALONIANS
1:9 ...................113
2:3 ...................116

## 1 TIMOTHY
1:3 .................... 60
2:11, 12 ............... 42
4:4 .................... 37
5:3 .................... 53

## HEBREWS
6:4-6 .................. 62
9:12-23 ................ 35

## JAMES
4:1 .................... 39
5:14 ................... 73

## 1 PETER
3:19 ................... 94
3:21 ................... 72
4:6 .................... 95
5:5 .................... 43

## 2 PETER
1:10 ................... 62
3:10 ................... 99

## 1 JOHN
1:3 .................... 60
2:1 .................... 69
2:12 ................... 59
3:6, 9 ................. 63
3:8, 9 ................. 69
5:9-13 ................. 56
5:16 ................... 63
6:17 ................... 67
6:18 ................... 59

## 3 JOHN
9-12 ................... 49

## REVELATION
2:7 ...................103
7:14 ..................109
13:15-18 ............... 84
13:17 .................. 80
15:2 ................... 32

www.ingramcontent.com/pod-product-compliance
Lightning Source LLC
Chambersburg PA
CBHW070458090426
42735CB00012B/2609